How Running Changed My Life

TRUE STORIES OF THE POWER OF RUNNING

Edited by Garth Battista

BREAKAWAY BOOKS
HALCOTTSVILLE, NY
2002

D0111839

How Running Changed My Life: True Stories of the Power of Running

Edited by Garth Battista

Front: cover photo credits: Beach Runners by Brian Drake; Long Road by John Laptal; Couple by Zephyr Images; Woman by Charlie Borland. All courtesy of Weststock.com.

   Back cover photo credits: Baby Jogger by Jacobs Stock Photography; Sunset by Photolink. Both courtesy of Getty Images.

ISBN: 1-891369-30-X
LIBRARY OF CONGRESS CONTROL NUMBER: 2002109908

Published by Breakaway Books
P.O. Box 24
Halcottsville, NY 12438
(800) 548-4348
www.breakawaybooks.com

FIRST EDITION

Contents

JOHN'S VISION	A. R. Ligon	9
RUNNER WITHOUT A CAUSE	Craig Boyer	13
DEAR DAD	Rita Stumps	19
THE RUNNER	J. Maxwell Cook	23
IN HIS FOOTSTEPS	Gerry Lavin	27
THE LONG FLAT MOUNTAIN	Holly Keith	33
ZEN AND THE ART OF MARATHON RUNNING	Matthew Strozier	37
RUNNING FOR MY LIFE	Erin Murphy	41
TRACK	Cheri Johnson	45
THE CIRCUITOUS ROUTE HOME	David Stockwell	49
RIGHT FOOT, LEFT FOOT	Karen Beuerlein	53
TREE OF HOPE	Vickie Bates	59
SUCCESS STORY	Michael Jewell	65
RUNNING IN THE BRONX	Odilia Rivera	69
SOME DAY	Beth Pollack	71
RUNNERS AND CHILDREN	Karen Kirkham	75
BEAUTIFUL GAZELLE	Abha Iyengar	79
RUN TO LIFE	Toby Tanser	83
ON THE ROAD	Ken Delano	89
FIFTY MORE YARDS	Walter Stoneham	93
WHAT *IS* SHE RUNNING FROM?	Jeannine Bergers Everett	97
FOREVER CHANGED, FOREVER RUNNER	Amy Abern	103
SIR JOHN	Muhammad Shehzad Hanif	107
THE TRAIL	Kerry A. Gildea	115
GOING TO THE CHAPEL	Jennifer Rucinski	121
A RUNNER'S EL DORADO	Joe Crisp	125
ONE BLOCK AT A TIME	Lori Dinkins	129
THE RUN	C. A. Robert	133

GRACE ASKED ME TO DANCE	Jane McDermott	137
LIFE IS TOO SHORT	Kami Holt	141
HOW I LEARNED TO STOP WORRYING AND LOVE RUNNING	David Barber	147
EVERYTHING I NEED TO KNOW I LEARNED FROM CROSS-COUNTRY RUNNING	Anne Thornton	151
EAT MY DUST	Kelley Leonardo	155
JUST KEEP MOVING	Joanne Moniz	161
RUNNING LESSONS	Kim Krolak	165
TOMORROW MIGHT NOT BE THE SAME	Mina Foster	171
MO(U)RNING RUN	Courtney E. Cole	175
HUSTLE	Matt Dinniman	179
COMPULSORY EXERCISE	Dean Liscum	183
RUNNER	Sharon Reidy	189
JUST PLAY	Christy Thomas	193
RUNNING AND WINGS	Sally Blue Wakeman	197
RUNNING WITH TIME	Roger Hart	201

Introduction

We've published many running books over the years here at Breakaway Books, and after a while a common refrain began to emerge: running will change your life. It seems obvious when you say it, but its full truth is elusive and profound. In our books *First Marathons, The Quotable Runner, The Runner's Literary Companion, Women Runners, The Elements of Effort, The Runner and the Path,* and John Bingham's *Penguin Brigade Training Log,* I kept coming across those words, either explicitly or implicitly. And though it's common knowledge to most people that running will dramatically alter your daily life, we'd never really gone much beyond the brief details to look at the large-scale changes, the beautiful human progress enabled by running.

So we decided to delve in: we put out a call for personal essays on the life-changing powers of running. The response was overwhelming: more than three hundred submissions came in, each with a clear voice and a moving story. Our judges read and read, marked and shuffled the immense stack of papers interminably, attempting to select a top forty. This book is the result. We had to leave out dozens of equally worthy stories simply for lack of space.

We even chose a winner, and a second and third place. You'll have your own preferences, but for the record Roger Hart was our number one, followed closely by A. R. Ligon and Craig Boyer. We've arranged them in salutatorian and valedictorian style, with Ms. Ligon and Mr. Boyer opening the book and Mr. Hart sending us off into the world.

I hope all these stories will be inspiring to runners of all stripes: old and young, men and women, fast and slow. And for would-be runners, I hope this book will send you out the door in running shoes. It's a long journey that begins with a single step.

Running makes you fit and makes you happy; it gives you strength and self-confidence; it occasionally moves you to extraordinary spiritual heights. For most of us runners, it will lengthen our lives, and more to the point, it increases the quality of every single moment we have here.

Running changed my life dramatically, profoundly, when I was an adolescent, and has shaped my life ever since. I feel I owe the sport (such a limiting word!) a debt of gratitude, and that sense of thankfulness shines through all the stories in this book.

Garth Battista
Publisher, Breakaway Books

If you have a story of how running changed your life, we'd love to read it. We hope to publish a sequel volume and are open to all new contributions. Essays should be 750 to 2000 words, with a clear voice, a moving story, and fine writing. Send them to:
   Breakaway Books
   Running Stories
   P. O. Box 24
   Halcottsville, NY 12438
   or by e-mail to: Run@breakawaybooks.com

John's Vision

A. R. Ligon

MERRILLVILLE, INDIANA

I always thought runners were the craziest people on earth. There they were sweltering in the heat of summer or soaked in torrents of rain, or worse yet, freezing in the dead of winter just to complete a run. I thought to myself, why on earth would you brave the elements just to suffer severe shortness of breath and leg cramps?

Then I met John. This short, funny guy with dark eyes and still darker head of hair. He was into fast cars, dance music, water sports, and above everything else was running. He'd run four miles, six days a week, religiously. I knew I needed to keep this guy's attention somehow. Fast cars were out—I drive like an old lady. Dance music was out—I have two left feet. Water sports were out—I was deathly afraid of drowning. That left only running.

My first attempt at running I did solo, so as not to embarrass myself. Naively, I wore my two-year-old cross-trainers and a flimsy old pair of socks. I ran as fast as I could from one end of the block to the other. I barely made it to the street corner with pain in my shins, sidestitches, and tightness in my chest because I couldn't breathe. It was a near-death experience.

I nearly quit but I really wanted to share this experience with John. So I got smarter the next time. I read books and magazines, and surfed the net for information. On my next run, I had a decent pair of running shoes on, a special pair of socks, and did stretches prior to running. I paced myself this time and was able to run farther with less discomfort. Before long, my distance doubled and I discovered the exhilaration after a run. That feeling of secret elation that you've surpassed yesterday's goal and you will always be able to surpass today's goal. The weeks flew by and I was running a mile to two miles. I was ready to run with John.

We met at a forest preserve with a beautiful trail. We did my two miles and it was unbelievable. I will never forget the feel of the ground under my feet, the breeze brushing strands of hair from my face, and the patches of light shining through the trees overhead. It was a communion with nature with someone special sharing it with me. I was hooked.

John and I would run at least three times a week from then on. On busy sidewalks, quiet trails, and the overcrowded lakefront. Looking back, they were the best dates I've ever had. No one had to worry about the uneasy silences or ordering the right food, and I didn't have to tear my closet apart trying to find the right outfit.

As our relationship grew, so did my passion for running. If I hit a wall, John would be there encouraging me. If I couldn't get up in the morning, he'd pull the covers from me and push me out of the bedroom. He became my coach and my partner.

Like all beautiful moments in life, the months flew by. The next thing that comes vividly to mind is a cold winter morning. The phone rings and it's John's mom, telling me John is gone.

"Gone where?" I asked.

"Gone forever, honey."

His mom proceeded to tell me the details with a choked-up voice. I could hear her but I couldn't understand what she was saying. I couldn't cry. I didn't want to cry. That would mean John was really gone.

I left the phone off the hook and put on my running shoes and just ran. I don't know for how long or how far. I just remember coming back home with warm tears running down my face, my lips cracked and bleeding from the cold, and hearing the busy tone on the phone. Only then did I let myself think. Of how John died. Of how he was hit by a speeding car as he was doing his early morning run. Of how he died before even being brought to the hospital. It seemed so unfair that the one thing that brought us together would take him away from me. I lost all my desire to run. There was no reason left for me to, and I didn't want any memory that would cause me any more pain. As a final gesture, I kept all my running shoes in my storage closet tucked away for good.

A year had passed and I was moving to a new apartment. I was packing all my things and inside one of my drawers I found one of John's pictures. He had his arms held high with fatigue and elation written all over his face. It was the picture of his first marathon. Right then it struck me that running was his life, his dream, and his commitment. He shared all that with me and more. And at that moment, with his picture in my hands, he gave me his vision. I wanted to complete my first marathon.

Now I train in any kind of weather and I brave all the elements just to run. This is for me and John. Maybe after a while I can put the past behind me and stop grieving. Maybe after a while the memories will leave and I can just run for me. But until then, I'm out there running with his vision. And you know what? I don't care if people think I'm crazy.

Runner Without a Cause

Craig Boyer

BEMIDJI, MINNESOTA

When I was a child I ran home from school, day after day, and I ran until my legs throbbed and my lungs ached and I fell in the wet grass along the railroad tracks. I rolled behind a thicket, hidden from the street. The blue October sky darkened and shined with the rhythm of my lungs. Time was short—they were coming. Just around the sunny corner where colored leaves were spinning, the neighborhood bullies were coming. I had to make it home.

But I didn't; I never made it home. And my failures provided my first conception of hell: listening to heavy footsteps and low voices while I held my quivering breath, while my legs throbbed, while the wind blew. The cold, autumn wind. I was only a second-grader; my pursuers were in junior high. For a brief season I lived a nightmare each day after school, but I got a lot of exercise. And I hated it. I longed for the day when I'd be bigger, when I'd never have to run again. Never would I run without a cause. Running when no one is chasing you is senseless; running *fast* when no one is chasing you is downright crazy.

I did get bigger, and no one chased me anymore. But somehow—perhaps as a result of those brief but unfavorable childhood experiences—I eventually went crazy. I became crazy enough to run for no reason, crazy enough to run almost anytime, anywhere.

When I lived in Arizona, daylight was all it took to get me running. Apart from the light all I needed were my shoes, a pair of socks, a jockstrap, a little pair of shorts and a bottle of sunblock. At high noon in the orange desert north of Phoenix, the temperature can reach one hundred and twenty-five degrees in the shade. The truth is that there is no shade. I smeared my body with sunblock till my skin shined and I ran slowly: I wasn't trying to deepen my tan or break any records. I only wanted to experience the desert in its foulest mood.

The mountains were red, so different from the furry green ones I'd climbed in Colorado. The desert forest is built of cactus— green-spiked monsters that have raised their heavy arms to this devil's sky for centuries. Horned lizards scurry between bright flowers strewn upon thorn-covered stems; diamondbacks warm themselves on blinding patches of sand not far from their holes. Powerlines threaten loudly above, slung between giants of steel. Hummingbirds swim in the heat, the absurd and impossible heat.

Six A.M. in January in Minnesota is no less absurd: I wakened in the dark and dressed in thermal underwear, wool stockings, three sweat-shirts, two caps, a scarf, and a pair of mittens. There wasn't any sun, and often just a sliver of moon. The ice and the tormenting gales belong to Dante: one morning the temperature dipped to twenty-three degrees below zero—crazy. And in Minnesota as in the ninth circle of hell, moist eyelids freeze. My breath turned to a fog that hardened upon my damp-ening scarf. Only the streetlights defied the cheerless dark. The trees along the hill I ascended were naked and black; a waterfall hid silently frozen deep within a narrow ravine. Sheets of ice lay draped over the sheer rocks above the sidewalk. The only sound was my footsteps, and the silence between.

Silence, however, can be a runner's companion. A true runner needs no starting pistol, no cheers, no noisy coach with a stopwatch, no *swish, swish, swish* of crisp October grass. A run is just the opposite of a race.

A race introduces the problem of *time*. And time becomes personalized, as in "What was *your* time?" Your time can even become your identity: in the sixth-grade my classmates and I were all briefly known by the single-digit numbers that straddled a colon. Rick was an 8:5. Kurt was a 7:6. I was a 7:8—I ran the fifty-yard dash in seven seconds and eight tenths. And I was hopelessly in love with a 6:9 named Nancy. It wasn't enough that I broke two minutes in the six hundred.

Nonetheless, I joined the cross-country team the next fall. The idea of long-distance running, however, still seemed a little crazy to me. On the first day of practice I noticed a strange newspaper photo tacked to the board in the locker room. It depicted a large group of runners, jogging in a pack. "This is gonna be easier than I thought," I thought, and I motioned to my little seventh-grade friends. I pointed to the picture. "I'm just gonna wait till the very end of the race and run right out in front!" I said. Unfortunately, I said it loudly enough to be overheard.

"That's just the beginning of the race, fool," said a towering senior, one of the captains. "Every race ends up looking like a string."

This, of course, is true. Though the first 440 is a squabble of elbows and spikes, the rest of the way—especially along the far reaches of the course—is a lonely battle, fought painfully against the self. But the subtle things you do out there, once everything is quiet but the staccato thud of footfalls, affects everyone.

By the time I was a senior I developed a strange habit: I laughed, like a crazy man, shattering the silent rhythm that prevails between runners in the lonely part of the race. I laughed as loudly as I could: "Ha! Ha! Ha!" I started doing it all the time. Finally, one of my teammates took me aside and pleaded with me in the locker room. "Look, I know the laughing you do is psyching out the other guys—but it's psyching us out too!"

I wasn't trying to "psyche" anyone out. I laughed because it seemed a natural thing to do. I laughed because I still silently believed that running when no one is chasing you is crazy. But I didn't mind if our opponents—and even some of my own teammates—wanted to believe that I was the craziest runner of all.

Years later, a quartet of silly teenagers in baseball caps arrived at the same conclusion. I was just minding my own business that warm, sunny afternoon, just running home from work at the lumberyard, my rusted Buick in the shop, my tattered work-boots slung by their chaffing strings across my shoulder. I didn't notice the car—a little sky-blue Datsun—as it slowed down and nudged up behind me. The next thing I knew, the passenger window descended and a chubby punk in a white baseball cap slopped his warm purple soda all over me. Then the car sped around the corner. The race was on.

They made straight for the stoplight and signaled to turn right. I sprinted across the supermarket parking lot, crossing at an angle, hoping to cut them off. I saw them turn. I wasn't far behind them when I reached the curb and I crossed two lanes of traffic without so much as a pause. Horns blared. The light turned red. The sky-blue car was idling about a dozen cars ahead, second in line. . . .

As I tore along the median I saw the driver's face in his own rear-view mirror, wide-eyed, acne-stained, frightened. I saw myself flash against a dozen mirrors: raging, shirtless, purple. My stride slackened. My boots slipped from my shoulder. I stopped. . . . The light turned green and they got away. I wasn't as crazy as they thought.

I am not a bully, after all. Nor am I some Jungian composite mixed from equal parts good and evil, lion and gazelle, light and darkness. One thing running has taught me is that it is no better to be the chaser than it is to be the chased: it is better to be neither.

My life is no longer a race, no matter how many casual, little races I choose to run. A starting pistol or a factory bell, a stopwatch or a calendar, a finish line or a funeral—it's really all the same. The most important thing that running has taught me is that there is Something in the universe stronger than time.

You can feel it at noon in the desert; you can feel it in the hours before dawn in frozen Minnesota. Singularity becomes solitude; identity fades to mere awareness. There is no chase, no race, no finish line. There are only sand and red mountains, snow and black trees. And somewhere in the brutal heat and violent cold there is a brief passage out of time—a silent door into eternity. A runner without a cause may be crazy, but he also might just catch a glimpse of heaven.

Dear Dad

Rita Stumps

VALLEY VILLAGE, CALIFORNIA

Nostalgia struck me recently, quite possibly as a result of my impending fortieth birthday. I don't usually reflect a lot on the past, but this upcoming event had me poring through old photo albums. The snapshots I discovered brought back vivid memories, long reflections triggered by the images preserved as a result of quick, flick-of-the-finger clicks on a camera's button. Most of the photographs were as expected: baby spitting up food, little girl digging in the dirt with an old spoon, young woman surrounded by brightly-colored birthday paper. Other pictures portrayed the events unique to my family, some of which I don't remember. I flipped through the pages of various volumes, remembering this and that, and suddenly came to a stop. There they were: a series of photos of the same young woman, dressed in shiny shorts and a tank top, bandana wrapped around her wrist, chalk blots on the dirt in front of her, eyes focused somewhere ahead, legs pumping, concentration on her face. That day sped back from its long-ago place: that morning, that cool fall day, the clear crisp air blowing through my hair. The ten-kilometer race in a small town, in the California high desert, that changed my life irrevocably.

My father took those photos that day. To my great surprise, that morning, when I got up earlier than a person should on a Sunday, he was there, waiting. Dad sat at the kitchen table, sipping coffee, taking bites alternately from a roll with jam and a softboiled egg, calmly reading the newspaper. He said he'd like to go with me to the race. Racing always makes me nervous, but those words made me more nervous than I'd ever been in my life. My father wanted to watch me run.

All my life, I felt Dad there, watching me like a prison guard, afraid to offer any freedom. The strictest of disciplinarians, he rarely smiled, and set detailed, complicated rules. He didn't seem to trust me. My becoming a teenager made life even worse: an eleven o'clock curfew appeared seemingly out of nowhere, and I suddenly had to account for every minute of every day. Unfair, I thought, especially since I'm an extremely independent person.

I had plenty of reasons to feel anxious that day, in addition to Dad's attending the race. The Apple Valley Pow Wow Days 5K/10K would directly benefit my alma mater, a small high school in a tiny high desert town. The people who volunteered their time came from my past— former teachers and local folks who had known me since the first grade. They didn't know me as a runner. I hadn't actually started running until college, long after the time of the quiet girl who sat in the back and got perfect grades.

As a result, skepticism surrounded me: "Your daughter is running today? The 10K?" No one spoke the words to me. Dad kept on his poker face, never betraying any emotions. When Mr. R., my favorite elementary school teacher, asked my father what he thought my finishing time would be, and Dad replied, "She said forty-five minutes," he looked at his stopwatch with great doubt.

You and I know that forty-five minutes is a very modest time for a 10K, but in a small, conservative town, where women don't run, forty-five minutes is an impossibility.

The race started. Some hundred runners participated in both races, mostly kids from local schools, in excellent shape because their cross-country season had started already. Most of them ran the 5K. The course was marked with chalk blots showing the way, and chalk lines indicated the mile marks. After a few blocks, I was alone. I could see no one ahead of me, no one behind me. I didn't know who was winning, how many women were in front of me. I ran for the sheer pleasure of racing against myself, alone with just miles of desert, houses here and there, and those inevitable chalk splotches. A mile passed, then two. I checked my watch for my times. Then came the halfway point. As I approached, I could see someone was there. A large pickup truck, a lone figure standing beside it, camera snapping away. My father. He was excited, shouting as I came near, "You're the first one!" The quiet, stern man I had known all of my life had the exuberance of a child at Christmas. He repeated, "You're the first one!"

The chalk marks indicated a turn in the course, which took me across sand, past tumbleweeds and Joshua trees, away from Dad. Still no other runners in sight. Miles four and five, and my old elementary school, came and went. The last mile went through one of the few real residential areas, so I couldn't see the final stretch, not until another, final turn. As I raced the last few hundred yards, toward the chute and across the finish line, there again was Dad. Snap, click, snap, click. I concentrated on breathing, picking up the pace, dashing those last few feet, just like I always do when I race. No big clock across the finish line, no broken tape from the runners before me, just the high school coach, shouting "43:31! First woman!" I said it was a small race, a small town. Women don't run 10Ks here.

Not that Dad would know. In his eyes I was like Joan Benoit, winning the biggest race of my life. I had to agree. I saw pride in his face, and in the way he strutted around, the man with the bragging rights: "My daughter won the race!" That day, and every day since then, he treated me differently. My working-class father never could comprehend doing well in school, going to college, the possibility of a woman being independent. Races are easy to understand: the fastest person wins. Strength counts, as does speed.

I earned my Dad's respect that day, but he also earned mine. In addition, I learned something books and school can't teach you: quiet people have emotions too; they just take longer to show them. People wait because they care. And most of all: I am quiet, strong, independent, stubborn. I am a lot like my father.

The photographs have faded and turned slightly yellow. The T-shirt has holes in it, the trophy broke into pieces long ago. My parents no longer live in Apple Valley. On a recent visit to their home in North Carolina, I kept up my usual routine, and ran every day. As I made my way up their road at the end of each run, I could see a man in the front yard, puttering around. I could see, as I approached, the same pride that began on a fall day, many years ago. I could also see that the garden didn't need any work.

The Runner

J. Maxwell Cook

STAMFORD, CONNECTICUT

Cold stuck around our apartment, oddly so, like it was an icebox. A thermostat existed ten inches above the dining room table, a structure that acted as a bookshelf in my living room, which happened to also be my bedroom. I checked the small box every five or six minutes and during commercials, calculating the impact on my natural gas bill if I were to nudge it in the direction of comfort. I figured, how much could one little nudge, really cost? But my thoughts responded, sneeringly, pointing out that one little nudge wouldn't make much of difference in temperature, anyway.

In the past, my living room/bedroom, could at times—especially when we were arguing—seem claustrophobic. But then she left me, and after that day, my place seemed big. Actually, for a while it appeared to me as massive, almost obnoxiously so. After she left, my place became a big, cold place.

I wasn't a runner. Not until the day she left, anyway, on that ugly day in my mammoth igloo of an apartment. As I stared at the thermostat, I was restless. My stomach felt weak, my skin hot, my bones cold. I'm not sure what I would have done: maybe crack a beer, search around for cigarettes she might've left behind, eat something unhealthy, or perhaps participate in some other, more personal form of self-abuse. But thankfully, an invasive idea took residence in my head. It sort of shouted at me the way discourteous people sometimes shout out in a crowded social engagement—with total disregard for what conversations may be taking place or what silences may be being observed.

"Run!" the thought shouted plainly, "run." The word itself was foreign. My memories of running were limited to the dreadful days I experienced as a child, running laps at soccer practice. But nonetheless the idea was forceful and oddly persuasive, so I ran.

I got off my couch and ran out my front door. The cold wind hit my face and I laughed. It was funny to think how just moments before I sat shivering helplessly on my couch, hiding from the cold. Now I was out in it, loving it. My legs moved independently, it seemed, like wheels in motion, and I smiled at the speed at which I was traveling. Immediately, I sensed my lungs, which felt cold, but healthy. The oxygen in my brain lifted me, and for the duration of the experience my mind was clear and free. I passed streetlights and dogs barking. I ran past a man scraping ice from his windshield, who waved at me with an awkward expression on his face. It was as if he was frightened, or maybe initially he thought that he had known me, but then quickly realized I was a stranger. I waved back and shouted to him over my shoulder, "Merry Christmas!"

He responded, "Happy Holidays!" which is something I didn't expect, but appreciated. I wondered what he must of thought of me, a tall gawky man in blue jeans and a sweater, running through the streets on Christmas Eve.

It became apparent, from my wheezing and shallow breaths that I was running out of gas. But when I thought about returning home, a feeling of dread came over me, so I kept moving on.

One unnaturally large snowflake fell through a yellowish beam coming from a street lamp ahead, and I raced forward to catch it with my tongue. The combination of my wild acceleration, and the patch of black ice under my feet, was a foul recipe for the achievement of this relatively simple task. However, I managed to get there in time, sliding on the denim protecting my buttocks and legs, and I caught the snowflake, as planned, with my outstretched tongue. The burst of moisture in my mouth was extraordinarily revitalizing, and after I recovered from my acrobatic slip, I had the energy to continue running.

But soon after that, my legs became jello and I was finished. Lucky for me I was only yards from my home. I limped through my front door and gradually crawled across my carpet and into bed. I slept peacefully and warmly for several hours. When I awoke, the first thing I looked at was the thermostat, and I considered the cost of nudging it. But when I looked out my window, I saw that it had snowed, and I remembered being a kid and the wonderful magic that came with a white Christmas. Soon I forgot all about the thermostat.

Yes, I missed her. But I rubbed my legs where they ached and I knew that I had found something that would never leave. I knew I could always run out my door and leave my sadness, or anything else, behind.

In His Footsteps

Gerry Lavin

SAN RAMON, CALIFORNIA

We were two of a handful of people taking a jog through a peaceful park. Birds chirped, trees swayed in a soft breeze and I wanted to throw up.

"How are you doing?" my father asked. His pace slowed to accompany mine.

"Oh, I'm fine," I said between breaths. "Feels good," I lied. I took another deep breath hoping my lungs would catch up with the irregular rhythm of my heartbeat. I wanted to add, "Is it over yet?" but I knew we hadn't finished the first mile.

Dad was enjoying himself. His daily run always made him feel good. I, on the other hand, had been doing it for three weeks straight and was still waiting for the fitness and fun part to kick in. Nausea began to overwhelm me.

"Running gives you a great chance to clear your head a little," he said with a smile. I was amazed at how he could run and talk at the same time. "A little mental fitness never hurt anybody."

Dad had taken up running months earlier to get in better shape. He was getting close to reaching the big 5-0 mark and discovered that body fat didn't just disappear anymore. The family was glad he was making efforts to stay healthy and encouraged Dad in his new hobby dedicated to his own personal enjoyment. "And as long as you prepare for it, like dress according to the weather and stretch out before you start, you'll be surprised at how far you can go."

I was surprised I hadn't collapsed and shocked I was doing any kind of physical exercise. I simply wasn't the type. My younger sister, Barbara, was the one on the high school track team. She ran a meet just a week before. Even my older brother, Steve, played Little League when he was a kid. I was the smart one, the bookworm, the homebody. I spent most of my time doing volunteer work for the National Honor Society and writing features for my school newspaper. So why was I kidding myself by pretending I was athletic?

"How far do you usually run, Dad?" I asked, trying to sound conversational.

"Well, on a weekday I'm limited in time," he said. "So it's about three miles. But if I have some extra time on a day off, I'll take it easy and stretch it to about five or six."

I was never so ungrateful for a Saturday morning. The possibility of continuing another five miles was unthinkable. My body parts were heavy and aching.

"One thing about running," Dad continued, as we trotted along a dirt path bordered by bright yellow daffodils. "It gives you a chance to notice the changing seasons."

Dad always had an appreciation of what went on around him. Almost every Saturday, when we were kids, he took my brother, sister and me on long walks through the Bear Mountain woods or other New York state parks, to give us a sense of adventure apart from the concrete sidewalks of Manhattan. He never pretended to know a lot about the "great outdoors." For the most part, our walks were quiet and unassuming. But we managed to stumble upon great discoveries like a gopher's hole, or a woodpecker, or an ill-fated tree that had been split by lightning. One time we almost tripped over a family of skunks and had to stop each other from breaking into fits of laughter while the mother skunk and her four junior skunks walked single-file two feet in front of us.

The thought of the skunks intensified my nausea.

"How are you holding up?" my father said again.

"Not too bad," I said with an enthusiasm too high in pitch. "How 'bout you?"

"Pretty good," he answered to my dismay, then proceeded to increase his pace as we ran one behind the other down a narrow pathway. My sluggish form struggled to close the expanding gap between us.

Why do people force their bodies beyond the point of inertia? Did people enjoy running? Why did I let my mother talk me into jogging with my father?

"Look at him," she had whispered in the corner of the living room after Dad returned from one of his first jogging expeditions. His face was alight at telling my sister how he had developed his own training program and how he had run two miles further than three days before. "He's like a little boy who just found a new toy and is waiting for someone to share it with. Why don't you go with him sometime?"

She was right, of course. Dad was like a boy in so many ways. Sometimes we failed to recognize it because it was such an inherent part of his being "Dad."

When we bought him a pair of roller skates for his forty-eighth birthday, neither my sister nor I thought twice about the eccentricity of the gift. It wasn't until my sister was driving home with some friends and one of them pointed to a fiftyish, slightly overweight, balding man with glasses gliding through the neighborhood streets that we started to think perhaps our Dad was not a typical middle-aged father.

"Look at that man on roller skates!" Barbara's friend declared.

"Oh, that's my father," Barbara said.

"Your father rollerskates?"

"Sure, why not?" My sister shrugged with a hint of noble pride. One of my father's greatest lessons was to believe in doing what you wanted to do, not in doing what people expected.

Of course, he was the last person in the world to be selfish about doing things. He was always doing what we wanted to do, from kite-flying to attending the Thanksgiving Day parade. He got a kick out of Barbara's friend's reaction to seeing him on roller skates. He laughed. Laughter came easy to him.

All of Dad's lessons were taught through time. We grew up learning how to roller skate and laugh and decipher algebra—not by Dad telling us how to do it, but by his doing it with us. Perhaps I was reaching the age of comprehending how far I had come because of Dad. High school graduation was a month away and I would be the first in the family to follow in Dad's footsteps by entering college. Maybe now it was time that I go out of my way to do something he wanted to do. Maybe I just wanted to let him know I understood how much it meant to me to spend time with him. If only my body would cooperate.

We rounded a bend that came out of the wooded area to an open sidewalk that continued through the park. Dad slowed down again so we could run side by side. My legs were lead weights in motion and my stomach was ready to turn inside-out.

"Any time you want to stop, just say so."

"Okay, but not yet," I gasped. I didn't want to slow him down, and the last thing I wanted to do was quit. Not now, not ever, not with Dad. I pushed on. My body cried for mercy. My mind raced in search of thoughtful distractions to keep it from dwelling on the self-inflicted physical torment. "How do you know how far you've run?" I asked between louder breaths.

"Well, if you run the same route every day you just compare it to the next day," Dad stated with ease, no gasping, no visible signs of nausea. "On days I'm feeling good, I take a little detour to add time, and on bad days I just try to cover the distance."

A sharp pain from nowhere in particular jabbed my left side. When would this end? Was Dad wondering why I started running? Did he understand what I was trying to tell him?

"Is this a good day for you?" I hoped held say he was too tired to go any farther.

"Sure it is," he said. We continued in a steady rhythm along the open path. "I usually stop at the entrance gate so I can warm down on the walk home," he said. "We're almost there."

Thank God. The end was near. I could do this. The invisible dagger jabbed me again and I almost doubled over.

"Remember," he said, as I struggled to keep pace with his seeming casual jaunt. "It's not how far you go, or how fast you finish. It's the fact that you go out there and do it that counts."

Dad had been telling me that all my life. He never asked anything of us three kids except that we at least try. More times than not, he believed, you'd go farther than you ever thought you could.

The entrance gate to the park was in sight, but now it seemed farther away than it was before I knew it was my finish line. Dad knew. He knew I didn't want to let him down by cutting his run short. He knew I was struggling, as I so often did with things in my life. He was telling me it was all right.

"C'mon, Dad." I smiled for the first time in miles. "Last one there's a rotten egg." I began to sprint and took the lead the last few hundred yards to the entrance gate. Dad came from behind the last few feet and beat me to the gate.

We crossed the finish line, laughing.

"You know," my father said, out of breath for the first time that day. "That's really not a healthy way to run."

"I know." My legs shook and I gasped for air once again. "But you didn't think I'd make it," I accused. "You thought I'd wimp out."

"No, no," he said. "I knew you'd make it."

And thanks to him, I always do.

I never stopped running after that day. Twenty years later, it's an essential part of my morning routine. Like so many things Dad taught me to love, running is the essence of my life. The most important part of every step is simply that I'm out there taking it. More times than not, I go farther than I ever imagined.

The Long Flat Mountain

Holly Keith

NORTHAMPTON, MASSACHUSSETS

Life changed my running before running changed my life. Everything changes your life. Running, bicycling, mountains. Rivers, rain, women, words. Every object, concept, person or gesture is a story line that changes other stories. In this story I am at the starting line of a marathon, my first. 26.2 miles. I had anticipated feeling relief at the finish, but at Mile Zero I am overcome with the relief of starting. Sometimes it's longer to the start than to the finish.

I am in high school asking our new coach how many laps we have to run before practice. She holds up her hand with five fingers extended. I think she is waving. Five laps. A mile and a quarter. Infinity to people accustomed to measuring distance in field lengths. We circle. We count.

I'm at Mile 2 of the marathon, along with thousands of other running people. There is an applauding crowd. I have never been applauded for running before. It's early morning. I worry about how to pace myself. The roads are closed. The highway crosses a river. For the length of the bridge I pace myself to the river.

The distance around the rural block I grow up on is 2.4 miles. I make this my unit for a run. Part of the route is unpaved, undeveloped, down through woods where the town's river overflows in spring. I have to tell my parents when I run the river route. They think the unpaved world may be unsafe, but the unpaved world is a reprieve, and fear is more dangerous than running in woods.

I'm at Mile 3 and the half-marathoners turn off, moving twice as fast for half the distance. We'll go another six miles before doubling back. The leaders begin to pass us coming the other way. Most runners are ahead of me. I define them as fast. At Mile 9 we turn back in the direction we came. Already my knees have forgotten the meaning of the verb "to turn." I watch runners behind me as they proceed to Mile 9. Runners behind me I define as brave.

In college I fall in love with a woman who runs. We run every day at dawn. Her job is to get us up and out there. My job is to keep us running. We run 2.4 miles for the 250 days we are in love. One day there is four feet of snow on the sidewalks, more in the air. We take five or ten steps and declare an act of God. It is beyond our control. On one day we do not run. On another day she is not in love.

I'm at Mile 13. I want to be at Mile 18. The plan becomes to get to Mile 18 and from there run four miles out past the starting point and four miles back to the finish. This is the plan. Not thirteen more miles, but two four mile runs once I get to the new starting line, five miles from here.

I continue to run every day, in all weather. One day I watch the rain stop and realize how many more times I've seen it start. Unless it's just easier to notice when things start than when they end.

At Mile 18 I enter the scenic mile used in pre-marathon promotions. In the artist's rendition, the path here is full of runners, moving at a fine pace, knees high. By the time I arrive at the scenic mile, the path is uncrowded. We are not lifting our feet. But there are only eight miles left. Four miles out, four miles back.

I meet a woman who doesn't run and fall in love with her. She bicycles and climbs mountains. I thought I bicycled when I rode twenty miles. She rides hundreds of miles. I ride with her. Bicycling a hundred miles makes running ten miles possible. She climbs mountains in winter. Climbing ten miles in winter makes bicycling farther possible, which makes running farther possible. Bike routes become running routes. The mountains get taller. The only thing that grows less possible is the relationship with the woman.

At Mile 19 I eat food I've been carrying. I've brought a hiker's mentality to the run. I have my own water bottle, my own fuel, moleskin. Volunteers offer outstretched beverages, but I am practicing self-sufficiency. Our route passes within shouting distance of the starting, and finishing, point. I hear cheers for finishers. I figure I have more than an hour before I can stop running. It may have been better not to have figured this out.

Mile 20. People are walking. I don't expect this. I try not to look at the walking people. I try not to be a walking person. Someone calls the incline in the road a hill. I think of the whole run as one long, flat mountain. You can't stop in the middle of a mountain. During training, running first hurt at ten miles, then fifteen, then eighteen, then twenty. The more you run the less it hurts. Running changes what pain is.

On a 130-mile bike ride I stop for directions. I tell the man where I'm going. He wants to know if this is my starting point. I tell him where I started, a hundred miles ago. He wants to know what day that was. That was this morning.

At Mile Indiscernible, someone says there are five kilometers remaining. The metric system. The distance remaining is in a foreign language. I do road math. I'm at Mile 23. For the first time I know I will finish. Imagine running. Imagine running farther. Running changes what distance is.

When I don't know how to take another step I imitate fluidity. I impersonate a runner. I run with my mind. There is no pain. There is no distance.

Mile 25. The Mile 25 sign makes me more happy than I am tired. I mean to be happy when I see the Mile 26 sign but at the same time I see the Finish Line ahead and forget the Mile 26 sign. The last 0.2 miles go by too quickly. I want to do them again. I want to do a lot of it again. Running changed my life. Something else will change my life.

It won't hurt. It's not far.

Zen and the Art of Marathon Running

Matthew Strozier

PELHAM, NEW YORK

Just after the start of the Marine Corps Marathon, I looked out at thousands of people running ahead of me. Their heads seemed to bounce in unison, and their colorful shirts formed what looked like a rainbow along the highway. At that point, there were 15,011 of us, most hoping to do no more than finish.

We were, on the whole, people with fading or mediocre athletic talent running far longer than is recommended by most doctors. Moderate exercise can add to a lifetime, but endurance competitors are not driven by a desire for a thin waistline. As writer Bill McKibben said of his experience with such training: "I came seeking sweat and found only enlightenment."

For the next twenty miles, however, I largely forgot about the runners around me, except to consider beating them. I took narcissistic pleasure in having people scream my name, which I had printed on my shirt, but rarely looked at the sidelines. I don't remember looking at the monuments that lined the course through Washington, D.C.

In the later miles, I still enjoyed the cheers but relished the silence among the runners around me. When we passed behind the Capitol, I heard nothing but a symphony of shoes pounding on pavement. Together, we were testing our physical limits, hoping to survive.

McKibben, whose training involved a year of Olympic-level work as a cross-country skier, described this type of moment in his book, *Long Distance*. During the course of his training, his father died of brain cancer, making him rethink the meaning of physical tests. Endurance, he said, became to him "a kind of elegance, a lightness that could only come from such deep comfort with yourself that you began to forget about yourself." I sensed that quiet behind the Capitol.

At points, I snapped out of this meditative state, sometimes for a laugh. An intense-looking Marine at the Mile 20 water station near the Lincoln Memorial, for example, shouted at me: "Go, Matt, go! Beat those guys! Trip them!" It might not be the cooperative spirit organizers wanted, but I imagine some professional football coaches say worse in locker rooms. I didn't take his advice.

Despite the ominous warnings, I didn't hit any wall in the final six miles. The trip around the Washington Mall went relatively well, and I crossed into Arlington in good spirits.

My mind, however, played tricks on me. At Mile 25, I convinced myself the finish line was at the base of the Iwo Jima War Memorial, not at the top. I sprinted the last 100 yards to the inflated red arch that had START written on it, only to realize I had another half-mile to go. To make matters worse, I had shouted to other runners earlier that we had a mile to go. We, in fact, had two.

At 3 hours and 34 minutes, I finished far better than I expected, but the ending was, to be honest, anti-climactic. No one shouted my name; the sound of shoes hitting the pavement was gone. I had no more hills to climb, no more early morning runs to dread, no more reward breakfasts of egg sandwiches. Life suddenly, shockingly, returned to normal. The first marathon of my life was over.

I walked past welcome tents full of food and sports drinks and circled around in a daze. Around me, runners stretched, hugged their wives and husbands and ate bananas. I couldn't find my family, so I watched other runners begin their ascent up that final, grueling hill I had misjudged just minutes before.

In the distance was a glorious view of the Washington Monument and the Capitol, which looked imposing and unprotected beneath a cloudless blue sky. The serene image was a stark contrast to the gaping hole in the Pentagon we had run past earlier where severed metal girders jutted out from blackened stone and a lone construction worker shouted to the runners, "I am proud of you!"

I turned my head and watched the runners go by. Their drama of pain—as McKibben described endurance competition—unfolded in front of me. Many had written their names in marker on their shirts, making the cloth look like an electronic news ticker announcing their thoughts. GO MARK GO! one shirt read. THANKS MOM AND DAD, another said.

The star athletes were done by that point and off collecting their medals. These were the survivors, the people who had decided, at some point in their lives, to complete a marathon. Training took them part of the way but desire had to carry them up this hill. Their goal was within yards.

At that moment, I felt the first shivers run across my skin. Cheering for these runners meant more to me than hearing my name shouted along the route. It was more inspiring to watch them test the limits of endurance than to test my own. I had run a marathon, I decided, to understand what those runners felt near the end. For a moment, I think I did.

Running For My Life

Erin Murphy

BARRINGTON, RHODE ISLAND

Running not only changed my life, it saved my life and continues to do so every day. I ran cross-country and track during high school. Those experiences were some of the best of my teenage years. A turbulent time which, for most of us, we would not care to relive. But if I could go back to the kinship and individual spirit of those practice times alone, I would in a second. I ran sporadically in college and for some time thereafter. But, eventually, the hobby dwindled as "real life" took over. I had never realized what the running had provided for me as I was growing up. Now, I consider it my greatest gift and thank God for the ability to run whenever I am appreciative enough to think of what my life would be like without it.

Now, I don't run because I'm on a team, because I'm trying to lose weight, or because health professionals say I should. I run, literally, be-cause I have to. Running everyday is as basic to me as breathing and eating. My spirit would die of starvation without it. Not only does it invigorate me physically, but it is also my sole time of uninterrupted contemplation and gives me the stamina to complete the other more arduous tasks of everyday living. In retrospect, once my running had decreased to sporadically, and then to never, I became a different person— of course physically, but also mentally and spiritually. After college, when I entered the "real world" I became apathetic, perplexed, and lost by its uncertainty and inconstancy. Because I could do anything, I did nothing.

I had no professional calling, no satisfying relationships, and most importantly no outlet for the pitfalls in life. I became lethargic and reclusive.

I don't know how or why but thankfully, by the grace of God or some other mystical presence, I rediscovered the gift of running. I picked it up again just as mysteriously as I abandoned it, and it resuscitated me. It provides a daily meditation for me, allows me to achieve a perspective on both the real and mystical world in which we live—a perspective I can gain through no other activity.

How to explain this to a non-runner? Well, it's part biological and part spiritual. Imagine one of your worse days in the recent past. Perhaps a relationship broke up, or you lost a job, or a child or parent became ill. Anything that caused you to re-evaluate your life and the realities around you. How did you cope with this incident?

I was certainly not one of the greatest victims of the September 11 attack on America; I was not physically close to either attack site, nor did I know anyone immediately affected. Yet, I still found myself paralyzed by it. I could only bear tidbits of the graphic news reports. Instead, I listened to the radio (briefly) in my room and cried in the dark—as if somehow the darkness would soften the blow. I tried to take a walk to clear my mind; I sat outside and stared up at the clear nighttime sky—but still my mind raced. Nothing seemed to quell my wild thoughts and emotions.

The next morning I woke up with the same restlessness, overwhelmed by feelings of helplessness. It was a sunny, mild day—under different circumstances it would have been a day filled with promise. But then it came time for my daily run. I have become what *Runners World* has termed a "streaker"—I have not missed a day of running in almost three years.

I had been staying at my parents' home in a nice community by the water. My run started slowly. Looking down and watching my feet hit the pavement, I glimpsed a couple of newly-placed lawn flags out of the corner of my eye. After the first half-mile I was sufficiently warmed up and my legs gained momentum, my breathing now rhythmic. As I reached the road that lined the harbor I no longer focused down on my feet, but on the setting around me. I now appreciated the view around me like never before. The sun was illuminating the boats rocking slightly on the water; the flags at half-mast in front of the quiet houses were flapping resiliently in the breeze. The sound of the ropes clinking on the boat masts and flag poles synchronized with my now lively pace. I took in the peaceful, and somehow brave vision and persistent sound around me, felt the strength in my legs, the smoothness of my breathing—and through running, found again a faith in myself that extends into the mystifying, sometimes malicious world around me. A faith in my ability to endure and rebound from hardship. A hope in the solemnity of nature and the divine possibilities of humankind.

I now realize what it is that running provided for me all these years. During those beginning slow, struggling steps, I am picking myself off the ground and wiping off the dirt—I am finding the courage to start again from scratch. And as my body becomes stronger and my stride longer, my confidence grows and I'm ready for the new challenges ahead. Crossing the finish line, as my adrenaline rushes and the satisfaction of achievement sets it, I gain a hope that greater feats can be tackled.

Finishing up my run on that otherwise somber September morning, as I rounded the corner to head home, I looked up to the sky and knew that, despite all the world's uncertainties, like myself that morning, we would pick ourselves up from the rubble and our country too would one day run strong again. I am as certain of this as I am that I will run again tomorrow, and the day after . . .

Track

Cheri Johnson

AUSTIN, TEXAS

Track meets make me ill. I can't even see the runners' sinewy legs, the bright fake grass, a soft sickening stretch of a long jump pit, without feeling a starting gun blast into my stomach. I remember lining up with the other teenage girls. We all checked: Were our jerseys carefully tucked, our legs shaved, our ponytails smoother than the next girl's? What boys were watching to see who would win, who would flop? Those girls' legs pumped sharp as shears. They didn't stray into other lanes, as I did, disqualifying myself by looking off wistfully at something else. Because things had not always been like this. I had begun running as a little girl, when I was so fiercely excited about it I could hardly think of anything else.

In elementary school we had begun to have annual contests for the fifty-yard dash and I decided to win. For much of the year in northern Minnesota the roads are covered in snow, but beginning in February I watched for patches of gravel under the grimy slush and ice; coming home on the bus I pushed my face into the window to see what bits of brown the wheels might be spitting up. As soon as I had glimpsed a patch of twenty yards I was out, slogging through the soppy dirt and rocks, racing the sorrel horse and timid cows on the other side of the fence, pumping, tripping, until the back of my throat felt as if it had been ripped into icy shreds. My feet were soaked, my toes stiff, but thrilled to be out of boots. Sometimes a procession of barn cats followed me out to watch, and I glanced periodically to make sure there were no cars coming to hit them. I waved at neighbors who came by slowly in trucks or on horses. In the quiet between sprints, when I had caught my breath and was plodding through the mud, I listened to the power lines hum and the crows caw, and I crept down into the ditch to see how close I could get to the fence before the cows floundered away in an anxious wave into the field. When I heard the muffler of my father's International, turning off the highway, I hurried back to walk in with him for supper, and we talked about my progress. My starts were quicker. I was pushing past the finish. I would be the fastest runner in the fourth grade.

Every April we ran the fifty-yard dash on a street near the school, and if I didn't get the best time I was close. After being on soft gravel running on pavement was effortless. Since the contest was only once a year I started lining up girls and boys on the playground in the spring and fall and challenging them to races. If I got beaten I tried the victor again; I was a gracious loser but a determined one. All summer I practiced through the long days when the sky stayed light until ten, as my mother scolded and said what if I got heatstroke, I wasn't going to like that, and I thought how frustrating it was to have a mother who was content to walk slowly through the pine trees with the dogs. But she had been a child herself, and then a teenage girl, and perhaps she saw where my zeal and competitiveness were headed.

She was right to worry. In sixth grade my pool of competitors began to dwindle. Some of the boys were becoming less graceful about defeat to a girl. If I beat them too many times they went to sulk and participate in mock marriages to more sedentary girls in the dug-outs. For a while I held out, pushing past them in the mud with my awkward stride, shoving my glasses up, whirling around to see who was next. But they kept leaving and one day I devised a strategy: I would let them win. For a while they stayed but eventually they preferred letting themselves be wrestled to the ground as grooms, anyway, and other more affable boys left too when I was no longer a worthy competitor. The girls had left long before to attend the weddings.

In seventh grade I ran with the track team but already I had begun to hate it. I was given a uniform and inherited my oldest sister's spikes but the exhilaration I had always felt in the line-up had turned into dread. I had let myself fail so many times on the playground I had begun to believe it was real; leaning over in the starting blocks I knew I would lose, and terribly; and no matter what, I'd certainly trip and knock over all the other girls, marring their pretty smooth bodies and long hair. I began to wonder: had I really been letting those boys win? Or had I just gotten slow? I began to feel awkward. My body leaned to the right when I ran, because during the day I carried a shoulder bag filled with too many books. I couldn't run in a straight line because I was used to swerving to avoid piles of soft gravel and sheets of ice. The other girls had fluffy ponytail holders that matched their uniforms, pastel sports bras, boyfriends in the bleachers, and little black purses, in which they carried tampons and birth control pills. They took hours to dress. I began to stray away from the track, lie in the grass, miss my races, and eventually I quit.

When I joined track I gave up running at home at all. I ran only in the line-up of girls on the track, with its strange tough sponginess, black with clear white boundaries. And now it still makes me sick. I feel some sympathy for my twelve-year-old self, bewildered, desperate when things began to change around her; but I am also disappointed in her for forgetting herself. I have never gone back to running.

But eventually I think I will forgive her. I am now remembering what she forgot. I take walks, like my mother did, and if it is cool or windy I sometimes feel the impulse to leap into a run. More and more often it's not the races I remember then, the uniforms, all those poor girls. It is a cold afternoon in March. Alone on a half-frozen road I notice the alfalfa fields are thawing, and beside me the young horse is pounding through the sopping grass and dirt.

The Circuitous Route Home

David Stockwell

SAN FRANCISCO, CALIFORNIA

For six years, I started every day by pumping cancer into my body. My lungs felt the warm, black inflation smoke seeks to fill, the slow drawing away of life, from life, before they felt even one breath of fresh air. My friends told me to quit. My parents were unsure whether to lecture or warn, as they struggled with the thinking that this was one of those choices their son was making—best to let him go, find his own way. Yet my father reminded me of my grandmother, and how he hated hearing her call from the kitchen, and he, placing aside the paper, walked the too familiar steps into the room where she sat, to adjust the oxygen. "Emphysema," he told me, "is the ugliest thing there is." My mother would wince at each drag I took, and allowed herself only the satisfaction of telling me that, at five dollars a pack, she couldn't understand how these people could afford it. I was one of those people. And I started each day religiously (and you can't tell me it's not religion—it has ritual, gathering, determination in the face of heretics; we were a clan outside of every building, and we stuck together); I started each day with a cigarette, my daily bread, waiting to be raised to my tongue like a wafer. No one could tell me anything. Even the doctor, who, on the thirtieth floor, in his private practice overlooking downtown San Francisco's Market Street, assured me that this had to stop. Even then, I remember the clouds flying by with the gulls, outside the window not far from the Embarcadero. Even then, as he tilted his head with that wise lilt of unfortunate knowing, and cautiously said, "Well, let's look at this . . ." I never listened. For until then, until he lit the glass frame on the wall, illuminating a square of fluorescence, and threw up the plastic x-ray into the beam—as all doctors are able to throw up an x-ray (perhaps you can even hear the sound now, flung upwards to catch the clip as it held there and hung)—until I saw the shadow, I didn't listen to anyone. I was twenty-nine years old.

I'm ashamed of what I'm about to tell you. As I was leaving the building, repeating to myself, "He said it 'could' be malignant . . . it could be malignant . . . Further tests, FUR-THER TESTS . . . Shit! Oh, shit, David."

People were staring at me. Rightfully so, as I was, at that point, a madman. I raved like a lunatic. Then, remembering, I felt their bulk in my jacket. A full, unopened pack. I jammed my hand down to rip them out of my pocket, out of my life. I walked quickly. A garbage can approached on the right. I couldn't wait to kill them, throw them deep into the can. Instead, I walked by. Put them back in my pocket. That night, I lit up and thought. Just thought.

So.

Running did not change my life. Running saved my life. I daresay it did even more than this; it gave me life. I know this now, but I couldn't see it then. Starting to run, to live, was, at the very least, an interesting process. Admittedly, the first day was easy, as I was more concerned with turning my entire life around in that first mile, trying to undo and erase everything from that day in the office at once; the stain, the memory, the memory of the stain, it all had to go. I sprinted out to the Panhandle—I lived two blocks from Golden Gate park (the Haight isn't the best neighborhood to live in if you want to quit smoking)—and felt myself running, running down. I did not have any energy.

One time the distributor cap crapped out in my Honda Accord, and the car simply wound down on the highway; I worked my way from fifth gear to first, then nothing at all. Dead. That's the way I felt that day. Dead. I say that it was easy, though, that first day, for I didn't know what lay in front of me, only what I needed to leave behind. And I was eager to take it on. Adrenaline rushed forward through me, giving me bursts of confidence, but I still had a lot to learn. I must have made it a mile and a half that August afternoon; I walked two more on the circuitous route home.

The second day was hell. I don't want to talk about it. The hardest thing about running is putting on your sneakers. Trust me, it's like going swimming—no matter how cold the water feels, once you get in, it's not bad. Best to just jump in. If I could battle my way into those shorts, tie up those laces, I was home free; it was as if I'd already gone running and the victory was immediately mine. Once I was ready to go, I was gone. But if I had to recall all those hours sitting off the side of the bed, still in shirt and tie and loafers, wearing my wrist watch and that tire around my waist, staring at those God-damn seventy dollar running shoes, staring back at me like a dog that wants to go for a walk, well, I'd have time for little else. (Incidentally, when I say "running," we both know I'm full of it. Really, I don't even mean "jogging." I'm not quite sure what it was I was doing. But I was moving.)

I take no credit for starting to run, nor for quitting smoking. Those same friends who warned me and reprimanded me, my parents who bit their tongues as they watched their son slowly committing suicide—those same people threw me parties, applauded me and saluted my strength. And yet, truthfully, not one pat on the back do I deserve. I credit the *distraction* of running, moving, breathing; this was responsible for my turn. Every step I ran was one less drag from the filter; every mile, one less cigarette; every day, ten more dollars in my wallet; every week,

51

one less carton. (You do the math—I was addicted, man). But, in time, the "distraction" became a new habit, a new addiction. To be honest, I am not now running 5Ks or 10Ks or marathons under three hours. This is not a "How-I-Overcame-Nicotine-Addiction-Beat-Cancer-And-Am-Now-A-World-Class-Runner" tale. I'm still an average guy who has, in fact, cut back on running a bit. I still head out three times a week at least, and last month, there was a fourteen-day period when I was out every day. But you asked me how running changed my life, and I'm telling you, it didn't; it *gave* me life. Today, I start each morning with the slow inhalation of air that all nature seeks. I watch the clouds flying with the gulls not far from the windmills by Ocean Beach. I listen to my friends, my parents, my doctor. And I'm going to make it. Home.

Right Foot, Left Foot

Karin Beuerlein

LORETTO, TENNESSEE

I would say that I'm devoted, but not devout. Persistent, but not pious. When it comes to that peculiar ritual of planting foot beyond foot ad infinitum until one sweats and bleeds—running, it's called now, because "jogging" is passé like terry-cloth shorts and socks with little balls on them—I could easily live without it, but I refuse to. It's like loving a dog that bites.

I came to the sport of running in a frame of mind typical of many women I know: I felt ordinary when I wanted to be Superwoman. I was fit but lacked that sweaty, sinewy meanness so obvious in the robo-babes of Nike ads. My flesh-to-steel ratio was a top-heavy fraction. While the distance a runner travels is trifling to an automobile, it was clear to me that burning miles into the soles of a woman's feet made her invincible. And leathery. With a body carved like a proud totem.

Probably, in a secret place I hardly recognize to exist, I even believed it would get rid of warts, spider veins, and gray hairs. If I were ever to get any.

There are many reasons why I should be no good at running. Physically, I have a few minor flaws that distinguish me unfavorably from my bronze sisters hawking sport shoes. North to south: White exercise mustache and pink exercise cheeks which falsely signal emergency to passersby. Narrow nasal passages and pea-sized lungs causing unceremonious blackout when overtaking dead possum and attendant odor on roadway. Uselessly wide hips through which children, as far as I can see, will never pass. Cowardly pair of knees inherited from gimpy paternal side of family. And finally, inch-high arches for which no sufficient support exists, forcing impact onto now-gangrenous balls of feet.

I'm also a natural pessimist; I can't fool myself when I'm in pain. I read once that when your energy is flagging toward the end of a run, you should imagine yourself heading for the final stretch of an Olympic heat, a world-champion set of legs separating from the pack. I've tried this. It doesn't work. Every time I head for the finish line, I start teetering like a Weeble, and Marion Jones appears out of nowhere and smokes my ass for the gold. Every time. I've actually had to stop running because of imaginary embarrassment. I know I'm not a world-class runner, and pretending I am doesn't make me go any faster.

So I'm not a paragon of endurance or an icon of speed. I haven't yet reached my goal of ten miles at a stretch; I have no idea how long it even takes me to run just one. I don't run in the snow or in 100-degree heat. My face will never assume the warrior-like gauntness of those who consider running their religion.

But I'm starting to figure out where my legs and my brain and my spirit converge—it had never occurred to me before, but they do intersect, and occasionally I can see the point in front of me as clearly as if I were graphing it on paper. It is both a place where I am and a place where I am going.

There is no typical day of running for me. Being self-employed, I can choose whatever part of the day I want to exercise. Theoretically. What usually happens is I grab the first half-hour chunk of time that presents itself and dart out the door before I can change my mind. Sometimes my mind beats me to the door and I have cookies instead.

Truthfully, running always seems like a bad idea until I am more than halfway finished. It feels like a bad idea while I'm sitting at my desk contemplating it, then while I'm changing into my sports bra and shorts, certainly while I'm lacing up my shoes, and more often than not towards the end of the first mile, when my feet feel like anvils. But somewhere along the way, as I'm looking toward my destination, the sweat melts away that core of doubt. It pours off me onto the road and I leave it behind.

Speaking of the road, it's not necessarily my favorite place to be. I live in the middle of nowhere, but that doesn't mean it's safe to run along the pavement. Although at first glance you'd think that running here in the country would be like paradise, but there are no sidewalks, and winding roads often conceal fiercely speeding pickup trucks until it's too late to dive for the ditch. Sometimes I run through town, where I am apt to encounter everyone I know while I'm in the worst state of pain and unattractiveness. More often I choose the safety of home.

Six-and-a-half laps on my long driveway equal one mile. Multiples of this one mile require a special tolerance for scenery that never changes. Even though the farm where I live is beautiful no matter what the season, the familiarity of the bumps and cracks under my feet creates a rut so deep I can lose my mind in it. Every time I set out on my own small journey, I have to find ways to steel myself, to make my soul as tough as my calluses.

Focused on the sound of my breath, I imagine the possible. As Marion will tell you on her way to the bank, the impossible does very little to buoy me. I'm a writer, and my imagination is broad and colorful, but I can't paint fantastical pictures when my feet and lungs feel like they're being run through with hot pokers. Instead, running seems to open me up to what is possible in my life. The farther I go, the more avenues roll out ahead of me, inviting me to sprint down and have a look.

Regardless of how hard my body is working, my mind focuses fiercely when my shoes pound the grass, tuned by the rhythmic sound of my breathing. I get great ideas for magazine articles as I force one foot ahead of the other. Phrases for poems condense from the churning word stew I keep roiling behind my forehead; thorny plot problems from my next novel lose their prickles and unravel. I imagine short stories selling on the first try. The bones of screenplays set themselves up in outline form against the blank sky, and I have been known to accept an Oscar or two in the last hundred yards of mile three. I did not say I was merely interested in the probable: I try to imagine the possible and take it with me, as far as it will stretch.

Some days, there's no getting beyond temporal concerns. When the body doesn't find a groove, the ideas don't come—and the converse may well be true. On those days, the effort to run is painful from start to finish, especially when my feet are blistered and I'm getting that snaky neck pain that feels like my forehead is tied to my shoulder with a three-inch cord. Sometimes I have to whisper *right foot, left foot, right foot* over and over again just to keep going.

But there's always a reward, no matter how small. I may not construct the perfect social novel by lap 21, but when I slow into a walk, my lungs stop burning and I revel in breath of a kind that I can't get anywhere else: fiery and full, it races all the way to my toes and expands beyond the reach of my body. It's a post-run high that floods and flushes. I crawl into bed later that night, face pink, knees aching, and one foot bloody, and I sleep like a woman who has no worries. Even though I have plenty.

Sometimes I can only run a mile when I wanted to go three. Sometimes I aim for two and get four. Occasionally, the plans I concoct on foot fall flat in the harsh light of the office, but some days they turn out to be gold. I have a spider vein right behind my knee, but upon close inspection in the mirror, my head still proves largely free of gray hair. I am sometimes more than the sum of my expectations, sometimes less than I wanted to be.

With each day gone by, with each footprint beaten into the grass, I have sailed quietly beyond the idea that I have to be a weakling or a Superwoman, one or the other. I am neither. I am not particularly sinewy or mean, but I am aware of my shrinking flesh-to-steel ratio, and not just in my thighs. I am an ordinary woman putting one foot in front of the other, every single day. Right, then left.

Tree of Hope

Vickie Bates

WOLFEBORO, NEW HAMPSHIRE

I began to dream about running after my back operation—dreams in which the knotting pain at the base of my spine vanished and running felt as easy as being carried along by a breeze.

I would wake from these dreams yearning to run, but I didn't. I was afraid my back couldn't take the repetitive pounding—foot to pavement, foot to pavement, foot to pavement—that running demands. I assumed the dreams fulfilled an impossible wish, my unconscious compensating for the limitations imposed on my body.

It's not that the operation was all that serious. It wasn't about herniated discs or pinched nerves or any of the things you usually hear about when people have back surgery. A journey by train through northern England and Scotland aggravated a small cyst over my sacrum, and it swelled to the size of a softball. I flew home for surgery, expecting the operation to take away the pain. That's when my real back troubles began.

Waking up in the recovery room, my head foggy from Darvon, I felt the first inkling of what was to come. The pain in my lower back was sharp and inescapable. Medication didn't reach it. The skin along my spine was drawn tight by the stitches. When the incision healed, I had seven inches of scar tissue running down my lower back. It took four or five months before I could bend down to pick up something on the floor; seven months before I could sit for more than a half hour; a year before I could sleep on my back again.

During that long, so-called recovery process my body grew constricted and unresponsive. I felt eighty-five years old. Over the next few years, I gave in to the inertia of chronic pain. I'd come home from work utterly drained from sitting all day. I'd fall into bed earlier and earlier each night. I spent inordinate amounts of time in front of a television set. I became helpless before "Nick at Nite," watching reruns of reruns I'd seen as a child. Once I actually called in sick three days in a row so I could be in bed and catch daytime reruns of "Bewitched."

For a while, the repetitiveness of TV was comforting. It kept me from having to think about whether there might be an alternative to the way I was living. At night, freed from force-fed images, I dreamed about running—splashing through the surf in the Gulf of Mexico; jogging down 24th Street in San Francisco; gliding between rows of eucalyptus trees—my back pliant, unencumbered. But still I didn't run.

Although the operation had given me a better sense of how much physical pain I was capable of enduring, it left me fearful of being in pain again. And that fear kept me rooted, frozen in my tracks, even as my dreams were telling me I was longing for movement, change of pace.

Around this time, I came across a painting called "Tree of Hope" in a book about Frida Kahlo. A young woman lies on a gurney, draped in sterile white hospital sheets. She is facing away from the viewer. Only her lower back is exposed, where two long gashes, like red serpents, rake the skin near her spinal column. It took my breath away. Like many Kahlo paintings, this was a self-portrait, but seeing it was like confronting my own damaged back for the first time. I was shocked at how much pain Kahlo had transmitted into the canvas. I didn't understand why she'd called it "Tree of Hope."

I feel I should state for the record that I never liked running. That doesn't mean I wasn't a jock. In high school, I earned varsity letters for soccer, basketball and softball. But I hated running. Laps and wind sprints were miseries to be endured in order to get to batting practice or to learn the jump shot.

I'd been an avid bicyclist, too. I've never been able to ride since the surgery, but if anything signified freedom and release for me it was cycling. So what was it with all the running dreams?

Finally, after a vividly transcendent dream in which I ran so effortlessly that my body took flight, I knew I had to face the fear, the wall of pain. I had to try to run.

"This is either going to be an amazing breakthrough, or the biggest mistake of my life," I thought when I first stepped on to a treadmill. I deliberately chose the treadmill instead of a track because if the ground wasn't moving beneath my feet, I knew I'd quit. The treadmill kept going and kept me going: I was afraid if I stopped I'd do a face plant and knock out my front teeth.

I was miserable those first weeks. I hated being out of breath, the hot frustrating pressure-cooker sensation building up in my chest, leaching my muscles of their strength. I could run for no more than a few minutes, less than a half mile. It took me three weeks, using the treadmill every other day, to be able to run one mile.

At first, nothing worked together—lungs, legs, back, arms—each part of my body seemed to move according to its own inharmonious rhythm. But once I could run a mile consistently, I started to experience the release I'd dreamed of. Gradually, somehow, the unwieldy and disparate-seeming parts of my body began to function as one. I'd still get winded, but it wasn't that scary gasping from deep in the lungs, when you can't catch your breath. Running made me feel like I was a child again, back in Maryland, where the spring morning air seemed weighted with honeysuckle dew, thick enough to float on.

Two years after that first run, my friend Alexa and I are training for a marathon and something odd has happened: I want to run. My desire to log mileage on that road to nowhere, with its "Star Trek" display panel, chafes against my running schedule, which dictates at least one day off between runs.

Recently, I had to scale back my schedule to allow a calf muscle injury the time it needs to recover. The muscle has been like a tight ball of rubber bands just below the back of my knee. In order to coax it to unwind, I have submitted to acupuncture treatments, even though I am so nervous around needles that acupuncture would be the torture served up to me in George Orwell's Room 101. Since the injury doesn't hurt, I run and ice the leg, run and ice, run and ice.

These workouts have transformed my body in ways I didn't think possible. I'd always seen runners, lean and sinewy, and assumed they were born with that body type. Now I'm not so sure that's innate. Up until now I would have described my "type" as husky, big boned, with soccer-player thighs, Tour de France thighs. But, a leanness is carving its way into my upper leg, defining the quadriceps. My shin bone feels sharp as a razor.

My body isn't the only thing being reshaped by running. I have acquired: subscriptions to running magazines (though I still feel like a foreigner in this new world); two pairs of identical running shoes (one for training, one reserved for races); the new habit of logging mileage in my datebook; and an unnatural fixation on Gatorade and related carbo-replenishment foods.

In January, I replace my daily chocolate snack with two pieces of fruit. I force myself to drink four to eight glasses of water every day because without it the muscles in my abdomen cramp when I run, and each step becomes a stab in the side.

In February, we sign up for our first race. Alexa talks about running the 10K course; my goals are simply to finish the 3K and to run the whole way, no stopping, no walking.

On race morning the sun evaporates the famous San Francisco fog early, but the air remains crisp. Alexa and I take our places in the crowd behind the starting line. At the gun, we start to jog lightly, heading north through Chinatown, dodging the slower runners and the early morning grocery shoppers startled by this mob in lycra tights. Alexa, soon outpaces me. I run alone along the wharves, slowing, leaden. The road pulls down my legs like a magnet. Just as I wonder if I will have to walk the rest of the way, I spot the 10K racers rejoining our route from the longer circuit. They are steely, focused, bearing down on the final stretch, jazzed. I pick up on their energy and move faster.

"I did it!" I am beaming as I cross the finish line.

I get right back into my regimen two days after the race. A marathon is 26.2 miles and I have at least three more races and a lot of training to do before October.

In March, I take four days off to rest my calf, and all my efforts unravel. The physical therapist suspects the tension in my calf muscle has been protecting some deeper injury. I call the acupuncturist. I try to stay calm as the days go by, as my legs become soft again, as the needles pierce my shin, the back of my knee, my ankle, my foot. I breathe deeply and feel the muscle start to unwind, one band at a time, tiny spasms at first, then, as the weeks go by, big painful ones. I can't run. I can't power walk. All I can do is acupuncture, ice, spasm.

I've been having running dreams again. Grounded, my dreams have taken flight. Despite the setback, I know that when my leg no longer hurts, I will go out and start running again. I will work my way up to one mile, then two, three, four, ten. The injury has thrown off the timing of my marathon, but it isn't holding back my desire to run it, to finish it, when I'm ready.

I know this because when I was running, I did it without hesitation, without the old procrastination and bargaining ("If you promise to go to the gym tomorrow, you can eat this pint of Ben & Jerry's Heath Bar Crunch tonight"). I ran when I could have been hanging out with friends. I ran instead of watching TV. I ran and ignored the books piling up on my nighttable. I ran the way yogis practice meditation.

I know because I ran even on the days when running was frustrating, when there was no fluidity or balance to my stride and the clump-stomp-clump-stomp of rubber soles against the treadmill forced me to turn up the volume on my Walkman till my ears rang. I kept going when I thought I'd plateaued at two miles. Around that time, Alexa announced that, barring injuries, she was going to step up her training schedule and complete her marathon in July, leaving me to run mine by myself in October. For a brief moment, I secretly wished that a mild, not-completely incapacitating accident might befall her. Then, I went to the gym, got on the treadmill and ran.

Mostly, though, I want to get back that feeling of being alive and inspired, like the day I broke my two-mile stalemate, let go of the need to check the display panel and, unrestrained by pain, time or distance, ran three miles without even realizing it. On those days, it doesn't matter how far or how fast I go, just that my breath flows in and out, in and out, like a gentle tide.

Success Story

Michael Jewell

WORCESTER, VERMONT

Because each side wanted to win during recess, I was the skinny kid who no one wanted to pick for their team in grade school. To my embarrassment, my Phys. Ed. teacher, Mrs. Krogman, kept me after class with the overweight girl everyone ridiculed, and tried to teach us how to throw a volleyball. While the school emptied out for the day, we stayed in the gym, tossing and dribbling awkwardly back and forth, until Mrs. Krogman seemed as uncoordinated as the two of us, and gave up the effort, saying we could leave and not asking us back. In the summer, I refused to play Little League because I caught a fastball in the shins at tryouts, and I only joined CYO basketball because my Dad was a coach, and let me in for the last three minutes of each game. Add to this that I preferred staying home on my days off, reading my collection of comic books, or watching my favorite TV shows, and it is surprising I have ended up spending so much time outdoors.

Perhaps it started when I was twelve and made friends with Vincent Datillio, who lived up our street and could be so aggravating that you just had to chase him, to try and shut him up. You always needed to be especially careful around Vincent, seeing that he could turn anything into a joke at your expense, and then squirm out of answering for it. Even so, he was likeable enough, and I remember walking with him one day down North Avenue, which is the main road leading from our suburb to the center of town, and he challenged me to race him to the end of the next block, and then to the next when we recovered, out of breath and having stomach cramps. Before we knew it we covered the length of the avenue, running and walking a distance of about two miles, and over the following weeks we would try it again, adding more blocks each time, before our rest stops.

Later, when I entered the ninth grade, I heard about cross-country running at the high school, where anyone could go out as a freshman, and simply run around in the woods, with no baseballs, basketballs, or volleyballs included, a major bonus being that all participants in varsity sports were excused from their P.E. requirements. Around this time I started wearing my first eyeglasses, and suddenly not only could the introverted, skinny kid see clearly, but here he was, among a mixed assortment of potential friends and co-conspirators, meeting for practice every afternoon, and competing once a week in races against other schools.

The problem was, in my first year I consistently came in last. By the time I trudged across the finish line, the rest of the runners had their sweatsuits on, and my team would spare me a half-hearted cheer, while they waited for the scores to be tabulated. But a turning point came near the end of that season. We were up against Winooski Valley High School, our rivals from the next town over, and all at once I noticed my team members cheering madly for me from the sidelines. When I asked what was the matter, to my astonishment they yelled "Come on Mike. There's someone behind you!" hearing which, with an uncharacteristic burst of speed, I sprinted for the finish and came in second from last. Now someone else had the distinction of being the final person off the course. I had arrived among the chosen.

I wish I could say that I went on to become an Olympic medallist. I also wish that I had startling good looks and perfect grammar. But I remain contented with simple gifts, remembering that by my senior year I had improved to the point of finishing races in the middle of the pack, ending my competitive career quite satisfactorily average. Since then, I sometimes think about the boy who took over for me in last place, and I wonder what success stories he remembers.

Did he also leave town after graduation, finding a good job out of state? Is he happily married, with children grown up and living on their own? Has he saved his worn-out letter jacket, with the letter he earned sewn on the front? Does he continue to run to keep in shape, his doctor assuring him that his health is better than most middle-aged men? Possibly he knows such moments which many veteran distance runners claim to have experienced even when they haven't, and the elusive second-wind comes to him as an intimation of something deeper. If so, he should be envied or admired.

As for myself, I go on seeking and finding success, in the pace of my footsteps over blacktop, and in the rhythm of my breath as I pass through the entrance of the lakeside park, where I let the tensions of the day disperse. I run beneath the pines until they begin to resemble those in an actual woodland, unsequestered, unmanicured, no longer on schedule, one of them fallen across the path, and following the harbor's edge, I pursue my shadow as it stretches away from me, down the beach which lies nearly empty after Labor Day. Past the polished headstones at the Cemetery, and briefly under the shade of the rusted holding tanks of the waterfront gas storage area, I am solitary, except for the seagulls as they tilt and dive, and the tiny figures of a couple walking their dog further down the shoreline. The Adirondacks appear insubstantial as they merge with silver on Lake Champlain, their roots catching fire, and a sailboat glints in the haze, each moment my heartbeat unfurled, metronomic yet spanning a tenuous juncture, my body, a leaf twirling mid-flight, the passage of time, a contour of driftwood as it enters its own reflection. As such, I achieve a certain stillness, resisting inertia only with effort, but also more than alive with exertion.

Running in the Bronx

Odilia Rivera

NEW YORK, NEW YORK

It was the crack-eighties. The local crackheads around 183rd Street and Morris Avenue in the Bronx eroded our sense of community. A sense of community is impossible when a wiry nervous fellow wants to hit you over the head with a stick to steal two dollars from you. I saw once beautiful sane men and women fall into unforeseen sinkholes. Drugs and the chaos they engendered ate away at families, dreams, and my courage. At that time, all I wanted was peace, quiet, and tranquility. I was afraid of my surroundings. I grieved for all the lost souls, but had no words that could remedy the situation.

My brother Orlando recognized my depression, stress, and inability to take a deep breath. He encouraged me to run and meditate. When I was seventeen, I started running. Orlando taught me stretches, breathing, and good nutrition for runners. At first, I had to stop after fifteen minutes, feeling like a wimp. But within a couple of weeks, I upped my mileage to five miles a day. My brother said I was a natural long-distance runner. I would leave my building, 2324 Morris Avenue, at 6 A.M. That quiet hour released me from my fears. The burned-out buildings and people began to look like potential. They were in waiting, maybe about to bloom.

I began to detach from my environment without losing compassion for the suffering of my brothers and sisters. I began to see the flux in life: constant beginnings, opportunities, deaths, and renewal. This idea of

69

the cyclical nature of life felt as if it were smelling salts under my nose. I awoke from an emotional coma and saw my role more clearly. Before I could save anyone else, I had to save myself.

When I ran in the afternoon, drug dealers cheered, and occasionally ran after me, but they were not able to keep up. Sometimes, I ran with Toni, my sister-in-law, through Van Cortlandt Park and around the reservoir. Together, we became warriors: I knew that if someone tried to hurt me, Toni would not run off to look for a telephone. She would say, "Screw that! I am 911!" We would fight together. We loved our fierceness and determination, peeping at our reflection in store windows on Fordham Road to admire our muscular legs.

Running through the Bronx is a visceral memory that will always live within me: cold mornings, lavender sky, the hallway in my building that served as shelter for drug addicts, the "body memory" of climbing the tough hills fluttering in my chest, my mother's admonitions to avoid cross-country running by myself, my nervous breaths and heavy stomps on long cross country runs by myself, Toni whining that 6 A.M. was too early, the naked man who jumped out of the woods in Van Cortlandt Park to yell at us.

And all those dreams that became unknotted in my mind took on life, all those dreams that became smooth as a road with challenging hills, all those dreams realized with the patience and determination gained through running in the Bronx.

Some Day

Beth Pollack

SKOKIE, ILLINOIS

"Some day, Bethie, I will run. Some day, Bethie, some day I will run."

Almost a century ago, she did. My grandmother grew up in a small village in Czechoslovakia, a tiny, vibrant girl who ran through the sprawling fields of Europe near her small farming town as she dreamed of so much in life yet to come. As the wild growth of the fields and paths of her world yielded to her pattering footsteps and sprang her forward into the crisp, clean village air, she thought of nothing but her goals in life, the things she wished to achieve and become, the family she wished to always hold dear, and the far off horizons she yearned to reach. Work around the farm and hardships could all be forgotten in her fields. In the mind of my bright-eyed, youthful, grandmother aspirations seemed only an arms length away. All she had to do was run further, hold out her hand, open her palm. . . .

And then, World War II snatched it all away. A concentration camp separated her from her life, dreams, family, and of course, her fields. Much of her family perished during those years in the camps, and along with them went her hope, innocence, youth, and most of her dreams. Yet my grandmother would simply not let the Nazis take her life. With an iron will and energy that she had always been known for, she vowed to keep her existence. The Nazis could take what they could, but they could never take her spirit; and when she was finally liberated from the camp years later, that was basically all that she had left. Her physical condition was poor, and most of her family and worldly possessions no longer existed, but she was determined to not let that stop her. One day she would return to her old life. One day she would run again and know that it was all in her reach.

Decades later, that day is still yet to come. She was driven from her old village when she tried to return after the war, and was forced to move her life to the bustling cities of America where her childhood fields and dreams were nothing but a distant gleam in her mind's eye. She also never fully physically recovered from what she went through in the camps. It has often broken my heart to see her, that same spark in her eyes, the same tenacious look that had always been rumored to never have left her face, but with swollen feet attached to her aging figure that could barely carry her from one room to the next, let alone run. Yet she still told me of her childhood, and of her fields, and whispered to me with a far-off look in her eyes, "Some day, Bethie, I will run. These feet cannot stop me forever. I will be strong yet. Some day, Bethie, some day I will run."

Hours turned into days, days turned into months, months turned into years and still she hobbled from room to room in her apartment and demanded that the day would come. It took me years before I could no longer bear to see her pain, and finally had to do something about it. Things were very confusing at that time in my life as a blossoming young woman, as I prepared to leave high school and make decisions about what I wanted to pursue in my future. Many of the things that I wanted to go after were scoffed at by other people as being unrealistic "dreams." People insisted that they were job fields that I would never make money in or be able to be successful in. I was told that I would regret my decision in the future. But something in my heart just did not want to let its innermost desires go in favor of the safe route. Something in me just needed more.

And so I ran.

I ran, and I ran and I ran. I laced up my shoes at sunrise on one blustery Chicago winter morning, threw on a few sweatshirts, and headed out into the streets of my small suburb of the city of Chicago. At first I did not understand what was so special about this seemingly innocent activity that captivated my grandmother as if it was the grandest gift that G-d had ever given us. But as the snow blanketed the peaceful earth around me, the morning sun shone down on my face, and as the world looked for a moment like a peaceful baby in its early morning sleep, my pace got faster and my pulse quickened. As the smooth snow and ice of my world yielded to my pattering footsteps and sprang me forward into the crisp but not-so-clean suburban air, I started to think of my goals and dreams in life. Parking lots have taken the place of fields, and rolling meadows might have been replaced by a thick wall of factories and stores, but decades later, thousands of miles, countries and what seemed like lifetimes away, I felt what my grandmother had felt as a child in the old country. I felt the world within my grasp on that cool morning. The wind whipped against my face as I strode faster through the quiet streets, but seemed to promise in its howl that nothing was impossible. Fresh snow covered my tracks and seemed to indicate that the past could always be overcome and forgotten if you were ready to put it behind you. I knew then that it was not only I who ran that morning. It was the spirit of my Grandmother right there beside me, and the hopes and aspirations of her and her family that had never been fully reached. I felt the burden of a lost generation on my bundled-up shoulders that morning, but carried it with me as I flew across the sidewalks of my world as if on fire. The desire was ignited in me in those wee hours to never let anything stop me and to always strive to reach my goals. After all, not everyone in this world had the opportunity to do so. Life was for living, and we only get one chance.

And if I ever forgot the message, I promised myself that I would run. I would run through the wind, wherever I might find myself, be it fields or factory lots, hills or alongside highways.

And I have run ever since. No matter the weather, no matter my mindset, I lace up my gym shoes and take my soul for a workout. And as the days go on and her legs get worse my grandmother still looks me in the eye and declares in utter seriousness, "Some day, Bethie, I will run. Some day, Bethie, some day I will run."

I pray every day that she will.

But until then her spirit is welcome to remain forever soaring next to me as the world lays peacefully asleep behind me and life's road lies open before me as I fly by . . .

How did running change my life? Simple. It made it begin.

Runners and Children

Karen Kirkham

I saw snow, for the first time, last winter. That may not seem like a big deal, but it is. You see, I've lived in Canada all my life. That adds up to forty-four winters. Forty-four cold, icy, snowy, winters. And although I have grown up in this climate, not until I began my journey as a runner did I really *see* snow.

My reason for incorporating running into my daily life had nothing to do with snow. I began running a few years ago for the same reason many other people start. I was looking for a way to lose weight. I had yo-yo dieted and struggled with the same fifteen pounds for years. I had tried, unsuccessfully, to add exercise to my diet regime, but exercise was never my friend. We quickly parted ways every time. I had tried weights, exercise bikes, and rowing machines. Despite the initial enthusiasm, I always packed it in within six weeks. I really hated exercising. I was reading an article one day about the many benefits of running, and the thing that interested me about it was the promise of lost fat and increased metabolism. A part of me knew that this would be a short-lived venture, just like all the other exercise routines that I had started, but I decided to give it a try too.

I sit here now, fifteen months later, and try to explain how it is that I am still running. My own family can't believe that I have stayed with it this long, but nobody is more surprised than I am. I have spent my adult life moving only as much as I had to. House to car. Car to house. Now, not only do I run, but I bicycle and walk too. I'm thinking of buying a pair of snowshoes this winter. But running is my favorite. Have I found the secret to a perfect figure? Am I finally at my ideal weight? No. I haven't lost any substantial amount of weight. Nor has my figure changed in any appreciable way. What has changed is *me*.

On my way to looking for a quick fix to my physical self, I found, quite by accident, a part of my being that had been lost for years. At what age did I cease to notice the beauty of nature around me?

Why did I no longer stop and smell the roses? It had been years since I had picked up a maple leaf, and pressed it between the pages of a book, like I did as a child. When did I start to see fallen oak and maple leaves as a nuisance, a chore for the weekend? It's all out there, and it's free. Virtual reality? How about the *real* thing? Fresh cut grass. Bare branches on trees. The smell of rain. River rock. Moss. Butterflies. I have now discovered bike paths, fields, and parks, where I once only knew of roads. Hills have become meaningful. I have felt the wonder of running among falling snowflakes on a still winter night, when homes are aglow with festive lights of the Christmas season. The sense of solitude and peace is indescribable. I run along, and wonder why so many people are sitting indoors, when there is so much beauty outside.

When I run in rain or snow, I often notice that the only ones I see outside are children, or other runners.

I think the key to my happiness is that I have rediscovered some of the joy of childhood. Running gives an adult an excuse to be out in the rain. When was the last time that you saw a non-running adult jumping over puddles? It is such a carefree exercise, how can you *not* feel like a child? I often wonder if the runners that I pass are in a battle with their stopwatch, a battle with their weight, or are just like me, running because it makes them feel like a kid. Running because it gives them a reason to be outside. After all the daily 'adult' duties are done, you can head outside and run. Hide your child-like bliss behind serious adult-looking running gear.

I admit that I have entered races. It's a wonderful opportunity to meet other runners, and soak up the great atmosphere. I will never win anything. I am notoriously slow. But I don't worry about that. I still don't have that lean runner's physique, and I likely never will. It is no longer a priority of mine. I have reaped the benefits of my healthier lifestyle, and my cholesterol levels are evidence of that. And that is a bonus. Sure I'd like to drop a few pounds, but I was mistaken to equate weight with happiness. So many of us fall into that trap. I have weighed less before than I do now, but I have never been happier than I am today. I feel positive and refreshed. I smile more. I am kinder. Despite the demands of a busy lifestyle, I feel grateful—thankful that I can play outside, in sun, rain, and snow.

Beautiful Gazelle

Abha Iyengar

DELHI, INDIA

I

There is a time when running and jumping and playing is all that you think of, and all that you do really. Then comes a time when sleeping, eating and routine housework is all that you do or think of really. If you are lucky, this is followed by a time when you catch yourself by the scruff of your collar, and decide to pull yourself out of the rut. It is not easy though.

First, you realize that you are too steeped in the habits that strive to make a couch potato out of you. Second, you realize that you have no extra money to burn to help you ignite a new path for yourself. Third, you realize that others who demand your time will not willingly make the required adjustments.

So, what do you do?

Well, I could have decided to let things ride, sobbed a bit, cursed my fate, and carried on with my fat, uncomfortable and mundane existence. But I decided to run instead. Not run from my life, but run for my life.

II

The first evening I took time out for myself, wore a track suit, put on a pair of ordinary Keds, tied my hair back, and stepped outside the door before my nerves failed me. There is no comfortable walking area around, except the paved path bordering the apartments where I live. If I step out of the main gates, I come on to a main traffic road. So, I decided to start off by doing rounds of the area around the building. This paved path is pleasant enough, its monotony broken by the shrubs and trees planted along one of its sides.

As I started running, the startled faces of my neighbors, out for their evening stroll, left an indelible impression on my mind. As I was fat and middle-aged, my initial run was more of an impossible trot, but I was not willing to get waylaid and give explanations to anyone. Within ten minutes I was sweating, aching, huffing and puffing, and wondering what in heaven's name had prompted me. I could only imagine what my neighbors would be thinking. Gone quite batty, they must have thought.

III

The next evening I was looking for excuses not to run. My legs didn't just ache, they felt like dead weights that were separate from the rest of my body, and which I was being forced to lug around. I just wanted to sit in front of the boob tube and lose myself in some inane serial.

"Who needs to go running?" I said. "I'm quite alright the way I am."

"You better go for your run, Mom," said my teenage son. "You need it!" He laid undue stress on the last three words. I had to get up and go. I could not give up now. At least I was garnering much needed family support.

Thus began a ritual of running from which I found no escape at first; then it became a part of my life.

IV

Over time, the experience of running changed for me.

At the beginning, it was the stiff-legged, painful attempts of a tired, unused body. It was like a creaking, rusted machine, which when suddenly started, splutters and shakes in protest. Gradually, with effort and *tapasya* (a Hindi word denoting discipline akin to prayer), my movements became less jagged, and more synchronized.

My legs still don't work with the speed of a well-oiled piston engine or the effortless ease of a ten year old, but I have no complaints. As long as I keep running, I know I'll get there. Meanwhile, the rhythm of my run exults me.

V

The experience of running then changed me.

As my running improved, I got less involved in its mechanics and more in my thoughts. In the beginning, I carried to my run the everyday problems; the agitations of my world. These would stay with me for quite a while. Slowly and gradually, my mind began to think of other things. It started veering toward thoughts that were philosophical. Then, as my running improved, so did my thinking. Gently, the cobwebs were getting cleared away. Quietness and peace began to descend on me.

While running I'm in a state of *sanyas*, which means "a disassociation with the irrelevant within and without." I leave all my cares and worries behind, as the wind whips my hair and cools my skin. I breathe deep and smell the jasmine in the air. The smooth, white, flowering magnolia blossoms delight my senses. Nature and mother earth and I are one.

VI

For many years, I had carried a weight not only on my body but also on my mind. Running made me fitter, healthier, and more cheerful. I became more carefree and spirited, willing to savor the moment.

It helped me to think, to find my space. It has been a catalyst of growth.

There is no music sweeter to me than the sound of my feet pounding their song on the ground, no high greater than what I get by feeling the rivulets of sweat pouring down my back. I am in communion with God. I am finding myself.

VII

"The journey of a thousand leagues begins with a single step," said Lao Tzu. My first run was the beginning of my liberation.

As I stand poised, in the light of the setting sun, I feel like a gazelle, bright-eyed and beautiful, dainty of feet and light of step. I am truly transformed.

Run to Life

Toby Tanser

NEW YORK, NEW YORK

The dark room filled with swirls of tobacco smoke, the curtains were drawn but the day was open. I tugged the Marlboro away from my upper lip as I felt the skin dry on the filter, and I automatically took a sip of Guinness to moisten my lips. She changed the channel, again.

I recognized him instantly. "Stop, wait! It's Carl Thackerey!" She was not really interested but inquired anyway, so I elaborated in excitement, "When I was a boy he used to be the top runner in a local club. I ran with him for a few training runs although he was older than me."

She looked across at me with an incredulous disbelieving expression, "You? Mr. Forty-Per-Day—a runner?" She broke into laughter, the sound rattled over a hoarse smokers' cough like coins through a coffee grinder.

At that moment I disliked her more than I had done for quite some time. I was in a rut like a slug in a slime jar. A month earlier, at her insistence, we had moved out of a one-bedroom apartment to rent a house with multiple bedrooms—for the two of us. She thought space would save our sinking relationship. We soon moved into separate bedrooms.

Where had I gone wrong? I stopped running, after a one year career that took me to state championships heights, because of knee trouble at the tender age of thirteen. Since that year I had become deeply involved in theater, motorcycles, and drinking beer. Of course smoking was thrown in. Everyone on the stage had to smoke.

I knew smoking was bad for me. I had tried numerous times to quit over the last six years. I had carried a bag of carrots for finger association, made monetary bets I could not afford to lose, and even hidden in closets and smoked in the dark. Nothing worked. I was hooked. Each morning when I awoke I had to grasp in the morning's blindness for my packet of cigarettes to light up the day.

My hand crumpled the cigarette packet as Thackerey ran away with a fine marathon performance representing his country. The women's race began. Scores of beautiful women toed the starting line, their Amazon bodies bronzed. I glanced over towards my girlfriend. She back at me. The cigarette packet flew into the garbage bin in the corner of the room.

I went up to the bathroom, I locked the door and jogged in place. The following day I purchased a cheap pair of running shoes. I waited until the cover of night, then I ran as fast as I could to the park, my waist-length hair streaming behind me.

Two months later I sat in a downtown bar in Reykjavík, Iceland. My cousin, Kristinn Hrafnsson, boasted of his physical fitness despite continuing to smoke. There was a race in one month. He wanted to challenge me. Beer would be the wager. In Iceland with beer at over ten dollars a glass, this was something to run for.

As the gun fired I shot into action. The race was 7K, and exactly how far that was, I wasn't too sure. A marathon and half marathon were being run in conjunction with my event. I sprinted to the front of the field—a place I had left behind nine years ago.

Two days later I had my chest X-rayed. The nurse looked with dismay at the X-ray, "You have the lungs of a fifty-year old man. You should stop smoking." She exclaimed. I pointed to my picture in the national newspaper breaking the tape and told her I was a runner. She double checked the spelling of the name, peering with disbelief.

A couple of years later and I was living in Stockholm. I belonged to an elite racing team, and we were undergoing physical tests. The size of my lungs was being measured, a test called Max VO_2. My test recorded the highest reading ever seen in Sweden for a runner. The nurse told me, "You have amazingly powerful lungs and a heart, like a lion."

I often think of how running changed my life. Of course my health really benefited the most, but also as I improved I was invited to cities all over the world to race, I met the most wonderful people, and I never regretted the change in my lifestyle.

Then one day running saved my life.

I was in Zanzibar, Tanzania, for the millennium celebration. It was December 29. The sun was setting over the Indian Ocean, the sweet smell of spices danced on the breeze, and I was running along the beach.

My thoughts were broken as two men approached me with questioning eyes. They were dressed in rags and were conferring under their breath with each other. I slowed from my run to a walk assuming they were coming to ask for help, or merely being friendly. I was gravely mistaken. One man instantly drew a large rusty machete knife from his jacket. The blade was ugly and curved. He quickly raised his arm and in a nanosecond I realized that I was the intended chopping block. Instinctively my arm went up to stop the heavy blow. Blood flew as if from a showerhead. At that moment the other man took a club that looked like a homemade baseball bat and whacked me over the head with tremendous force. I fell stunned to the sand.

Just moments later I regained consciousness as they were trying to remove my right sneaker. My watch, sunglasses, and the left sneaker had already been taken. I sprung up and attacked the man with the knife as the other man hit me again and again with the club. Somehow, through sheer anger, I managed to grapple and grab the knife. I dragged the blade from his hand. Now the tide changed. They stood back as I wielded the knife.

They were very cross about not getting the other shoe but they dared not to approach me. (Ironically I had sent boxes and boxes of mostly used running shoes to East African athletes over the last five years through a program I had developed while in Kenya in 1995 and 1996.)

I was covered from head to toe in blood when they ran off. Not only me but the surrounding sand was crimson. My wrist was awful; I could see the white bone with some stringy things by the bone, I really thought my hand would fall off. With my other hand I felt my head and realized that my skull was cracked and badly dented. Blood was gushing out.

Oddly, I felt very at peace with the world and just wanted to lie down on the warm sand and go to sleep imagining the serene Indian Ocean gently bringing her tide over me. I was very close to doing so. A thought jolted my mind: *survive*. I removed my singlet and tied it tightly round my wrist. I then set off running, looking for help.

I could not see very clearly at all, just images of dull color. I kept blacking out and nearly fainting. However I could hear the sea on my left and I knew I had to run two miles to where the hired Vespa was parked.

Luckily throughout the attack I had held on tightly to the ignition key. I also had the machete just in case they returned. I ran like I had never run before, staggering like a drunk, scared that with my elevated heartbeat the blood would pump even quicker from my body. It was very painful to run. My head ached unbearably, and I had a queasy feeling that I was close to losing so much blood that I would faint and bleed to death.

I made out a big building to my right after quite some time, and recognized it as the old presidential building. The Vespa was nearby so I ran toward it, stumbling through a garden and some bushes, convinced any moment I would drop.

The adventure took many further turns as I struggled to leave Africa and my health degenerated. I was told by four separate doctors that I should have never made it alive off the beach, or out of Africa.

However, after brain surgery on January 14, and a short recovery time, I started running again—it was not long before I was competing again winning the Manhattan Half Marathon, and a host of other local New York City races. In the fall I completed the 2000 New York City Marathon, finishing 35th.

Not only did running change my life, it also saved my life.

On the Road

Ken Delano

ASHEVILLE, NORTH CAROLINA

Zero done, the starting gun.

Twenty-six, the run, to go with this one.

One done twenty-five to go with this one.

One done twenty-five to go with this one.

Well begun is doing the first one.

My running life, though you runners know it's my only real life, this week is twenty-six laps—twenty-six motel parking lot laps because, "sorry, but there sure just ain't no trails in this town, sir." Last week it was fifty-two; a smaller motel. Twenty-six laps because as you just heard from my motel clerk it's the safest (only) place to run in this particular name-withheld-what's-the-point-in-naming-it-it-doesn't-know-why-we-runners-spurn-it-town. But all is forgotten when I'm actually out here doing the run. Once these legs start churning there's no more reason to be spurning anything. All is forgiven as is, I trust, my opening attitude. Thank you kindly.

Seven done nineteen (less than twenty!) to go with this one.

Seven done nineteen to go with this one.

It's my job that keeps me on the road, never in one place for long. On the road. A runner on the road! So what's wrong with that? I *am* a road runner. Yes, there is the occasional treadmill I admit. Hey, it's late, and dark, can't see the ditches or potholes and the motel has no looping parking lot. When there is, I loop and loop and lap and lap and lap it up with a smile. I'm on the road traveling with my other love. It's my job that keeps me out here. But I'm fortunate because in no way is it work. I tour the entire USA (get to check out all the great running cities, and like tonight's, all the others too) with my wife acting out poetry for schools—all ages. I mention this because you the reader may need to know why and how a running-regimentarian can do it all without *the* routine (although I, anal retentive me, do endorse *the* routine). Acting is focused; so focused it helps the running. And the work with the kids is as energy-filled as any daily energy bar snack break.

Twelve done fourteen to go with this one.

Twelve done, almost halfway, fourteen to go with this one

It's a mantra. It's a mantra that changes. Well, it sort of changes. The numbers change. So I get consistency *and* I get change. A change in my life, my life's moment; that 'at that' moment. It's the one we need experience every day. I get change in one movement; one repetitive movement; one wonderful, wonderfully repetitive move.

Twelve done fourteen to . . . No. No. No. Thirteen done thirteen to go with this one.

I lost count. But this counting is how I keep score. Not a "who's winning" score, but a "where am I" score. It's how I keep focus. How I compete with myself when that's what I want to be doing out here and to know where I am. Of course when I don't want to know where or don't care I can make up the numbers. I can click the watch off and be Bill Rogers (I grew up wanting to grow up in and run away from Hopkinton) running away with my dreams of Boston. My dreams of beyond, beyond, beyond even beyond my dreams. And I didn't even know it. I remember seeing Kip Keno's smile on Wide World of Sports. (halfway there). Halfway from where the first step reminds me everyday of *the* first step. Where in my memory is that first of all steps? And how long was it before I knew walking wasn't enough? Where is the impression, that footprint on my memory, of that first running step? Or maybe the question is, "don't all children run rather than walk?" We're all always ready to crawl full out. No kid crawls slow after that first adventure. "Look ma, no knee pads."

Yes! It's thirteen done thirteen to go with this one.

My life it seems is always halfway done halfway to go with this one. This one what? Ever think about that? Aren't we always halfway to and from something? And can't we as easily ask, "are we not always fully there?" Or, fully here, fully present where we are and where we want (if we believe we have a say in this decision making) to be?

Eighteen just eight to go with this one.

Single numbers only, the last leg, the stretch run. It is here where the answer appears. It is now when I begin to know why I run. My mind can reason it. It is clear and sharp, though that is not why my mind runs. It is logical, but my mind does not run to be sane. It runs to be satisfied. And yet it thrives on its own insatiability. And my body, well, it will have to wait a while. But that's okay for it too (and it knows it) will experience, indeed fully enjoy the anxiety of experiencing the exhilaration of the endorphins. The body feels healthy, but no body runs this way to feel healthy. That is not why it runs. It runs because . . . it runs.

And on those other days when I'm halfway from, or to, "what am I doing out here today?" It is here where I can find, can remember, I can invent every reason to doubt. It is here where I can believe aching legs. It is here I can blame the weather, blame the traffic, the day before, blame the day to come. But when you're calling a runner who's a step to thoughtful step to waste at twenty-four two to go with this one? . . . What was that, that thought? It sounded oddly profound yet was making nearly nothing but nonsense (here I am again making nonsense out of no sense at all) and I've got to stay focused here. I do not want doubt or miscalculation to repeat twenty-four two or worse twenty-three three; not now. These laps, and we do know they may be miles, these are mine.

Twenty-five done and one to go with this one.

It is now I know I am there; from here I know this. From here I know I am already there. And all there is there, here, is running. So, I am the running. That's what running has become for me. That's what I have become. RUNNING! Not the runner. Not, I am one who runs. Not, my body is running because my legs are moving. This person, this I is running. And in these moments there is nothing else. No this and that. No other thing. No body and space. No being and environment. No separation. Instead, full unity. No outside forces at work here. In these moments, when I am RUNNING, there is no time. No fast or slow, no rate. And there is no resistance. No friction. There is no gravity. Yet at these moments I am as grounded as one has ever been. I am connected to everything. I am RUNNING. And running has become ME.

Fifty More Yards

Walter Stoneham

SAN ANTONIO, TEXAS

One Saturday morning many years ago, I decided to go out to the park here in San Antonio where marathon runners train, just to check it out. I'd been running only a mile or two on a local high school track for about a year. I'm saying "only a mile or two" because, at that time, I was an overweight cigarette smoker—had been for twenty years. After running a couple of miles that Saturday morning, I sat with others there listening with interest and amazement while they talked of their previous and next marathons. Driving home from the park I decided that I wanted to become a marathon runner. But to do so, I knew I'd have to stop smoking. Listening to those marathoners talk that Saturday morning must have really inspired me because, on my forty-sixth birthday, while returning from a fishing trip at the Texas coast, I threw away the half pack of cigarettes in my shirt pocket. Several weeks later I went back out to McAllister Park to talk with those marathon runners and begin training to become a marathon runner myself.

Eleven months later, on March 31, 1979, thanks to the training assistance of my new running friends, I completed my first marathon with a time of 4:08; not too bad for a forty-six-year-old ex-smoker. Finally conquering 26.2 miles filled me with eagerness to break the four-hour mark. So, with the continued advice of my more experienced marathoning friends, I intensified my training in preparation for a second marathon. October 27, 1979, I ran the Las Colonias marathon here in San Antonio; finished in 3:53. What a great feeling! I know just running under four hours isn't really considered a tremendous accomplishment in the marathoning community; but I was never a fast runner even back in my high school track team days. And my 10K runs were in the forty-eight to fifty minute range. So, for me, breaking four hours was a personal accomplishment of some merit. Next, on December 1, 1979, I completed the White Rock marathon in Dallas; my time—3:48. Wow! Then, on January 19, 1980, I ran the Houston-Tenneco marathon. Another sub-four-hour finish—3:51.

Training for and completing these three marathons filled me with a love for marathoning. I began to seek out more obscure marathons to run. Two of the six marathons I ran in 1980 were such races; the Mean Green in Denton, Texas, and the Davis Mountain at Fort Davis in far West Texas. The Mean Green was just that. We ran through open fields and across a shallow creek. Such courses produce slower times for all runners. I finished third in my age group with a 4:06. Got a trophy. Found another tough course at Fort Davis—out and back with the first half uphill into the wind. This November day the temperature was 33 and it was misting rain. Again, slower times. Trophies were bronze plaques in the shape of Texas with the Davis Mountains raised in relief. I really wanted one of those trophies and since there were only seven runners in my age group, I was determined to do it. Heading out to the turn around, I saw two other runners in my age group already on their way back. After about 200 yards or so on my way back, I saw the other runners in my age group heading for the turn around. Then I knew the third place plaque could be mine. I kept looking back and when one of the others got closer than I wanted I picked up my pace. That's the only time I ran the final mile and 385 yards in fairly serious pain. I got the plaque.

Apparently, Houston-Tenneco was my favorite marathon; I ran it seven times. Also, it's where both my fastest and slowest times were recorded. In 1983, at age fifty-one, I finished in 3:46—my P.R. At age fifty-six, I hadn't planned to run in Houston and didn't really train for the marathon distance. Three of my running friends were going to Houston and urged me to go with them. Although I hadn't sufficiently trained, I did have twenty-eight marathons under my belt. So I decided to give it a shot. Also, since becoming a trimmer, happier non-smoker nine years back, I lost twenty-five pounds and felt like I was in my thirties again. With all those marathons behind me, developing running strategies came easy. Four years earlier, I ran a 50K using the "run fifteen minutes, walk five" strategy. Finished in 5:26. I figured if I used the "Fifteen/five" method I could finish in around 4:45, even though I didn't prepare properly. So that's what I did and finished at 4:47; my slowest marathon. Ran four more marathons for a total of thirty-three. Ran the last one at age sixty-four. Then set a goal of fifty marathons by age seventy. I could easily run seventeen marathons in six years.

At age sixty-five, my dream of fifty marathons became something akin to a nightmare. While I was cross-training, the front wheel of my bicycle dropped into a semi-open drain cover. The sudden stop threw me up in the air, over the handlebars and down on my head, resulting in a serious spinal cord injury.

I was told a nearby EMS unit picked my near-lifeless body off the asphalt and took me to University Hospital. That's where I regained consciousness several days later in the intensive care unit. I remember almost nothing of the twenty-two days spent in intensive care, but my wife tells me that every day for the first five days the doctors told her there way no way I could survive. I guess an old guy who survives thirty-three marathons can survive most anything. Later the doctors told me the reason I survived was my great physical condition prior to the injury. Perhaps running saved my life.

From the intensive care unit I was transferred to a rehabilitation hospital where I spent fourteen weeks trying to regain the functionality lost lying motionless for all those days. The first three days, I was still too weak to get out of bed. When I was able to get out of bed with help, I was taken to the therapy room in a wheelchair. Therapy began with simply trying to stand. I remember clearly the goal of standing unaided for one minute. Next came re-learning to walk. At first, with a therapist on each arm. After a couple of days, with one therapist just walking around the therapy room. Finally, after several days with one therapist walking a bit farther each day, I took thirty steps unaided.

Because my injury was in the spinal cord just below the neck, my upper body suffered most; especially my shoulders, arms and hands. Therapy here was not as successful as that for my legs. I still have limited range of motion in my arms and very limited use of my left hand.

After fourteen weeks in the rehab hospital, I came home. I spent eighteen months in outpatient facilities and gained substantially increased walking ability and some small increase in arm and hand flexibility. Now my therapy consists of deep tissue massage and some work on weight machines at a local health club; the weight work to strengthen my legs and core muscularity. Hopefully, this will correct my problem with balance enough so that I can reach my new "by-age-seventy" goal: to go to McAllister park and run fifty yards. I know I'll never run another marathon, but just fifty yards is a realistic possibility. And it will allow my body to feel the wonderful sensation of running once again. Even though my fifty marathons dream vanished four years ago, I remain ever so thankful for the marathoning days I did enjoy and how running twice changed my life.

What *Is* She Running From?

Jeannine Bergers Everett

REDWOOD CITY, CALIFORNIA

We ordered weed-whacker salad and iced tea. After all, this was California. My New Yorker friend and I nibbled at what looked like the Roundup left behind and took up people-watching from the sidewalk café off the Embarcadero. That's when she said it.

"What *is* she running from?" My friend noticed a well-toned woman jogging along the bay. "She looks absolutely miserable." I laughed politely, but I felt something odd in my stomach. Given what I ate for lunch (or should I say, what I *didn't* eat for lunch) it must have been hunger. But the feeling dogged me most of the day. Could it be that California was sinking in? The reality was, she didn't look miserable to me. She looked . . . peaceful. Could I find that kind of peace in physical exertion?

Right. I grew up in the Midwest. Vegetables were something that decorated the plate between the meat and the potatoes. Lunch was not lunch without a Twinkie and there was dessert after every meal. I also remember playing outside, but I remember a lot of "Gilligan's Island" and "Kimba the White Lion" too. My mom smoked, my dad drank cocktails at every lunch and dinner and if you were over the age of ten, you just didn't get tennis shoes anymore.

Even worse, no one would ever claim that I was blessed with grace. My siblings used to tease—if there was an empty room with one stray item in it, I could be counted on to trip over it. I started to identify with

97

my non-athletic status, even wear it as a badge. I embraced more cerebral activities while secretly longing for more.

In high school, the track coach saw my sprint times on the Presidential Fitness test. Fast enough to make up for my complete failure at just about everything else. When I came into biology class (yes, he was the biology teacher) he suggested I come to practice. When the entire class laughed, I decided that this was not a good idea.

In college, I decided that I would let go of my inhibitions. I pulled on the shoes and went for a run. Not a long run (not very good shoes, either for that matter). I ran in secret for a week. Then I told my then boyfriend that I was going to train for a 5K.

All he said was "I guess they won't really care if you don't finish." Now that should have been the sign to dump the boyfriend. For all my talk of cerebral activity, I was pretty stupid. Rather than telling the boyfriend to take a leap, I put the shoes away. All I thought was, "thank goodness I didn't buy new ones".

Years went by and I took up a more balanced lifestyle. I even married a runner. But I didn't run myself. I'd try from time to time, and give up after a month or two. It just wasn't me.

But who on earth knows who they are at twenty-five? I'm not so sure I even knew at thirty-five, but I was more open to the possibilities. In my work as a researcher into human behavior, I was looking at the role of title and declaration on decision and action. In this work, I saw the relationship between open declaration and commitment to achieve— you aren't what you eat, you are what you say you are.

During this time, I met a woman who did research in balanced lifestyle and goal setting. She put me through an assessment that she found predicted overall happiness and emotional well-being. I did pretty well—I have a good life. Except for one area.

I participated in physical activity, but I had no goals. I was just working out to work out. Because it was what I should do, but not because I was trying to do something in particular. I was sort of taken aback. I'm a pretty goal-driven person by nature, but had no goals as far as my physical fitness was concerned.

I went back to my own work about title and declaration. We give ourselves so many titles we don't deserve—lazy, selfish, unworthy—all negative. What would happen if I gave myself an undeserved title that was positive?

At that moment, I became an athlete.

I asked myself, what would an athlete do? An athlete would run.

I went to a running store and got a good pair of running shoes and a reflective jacket. I figured out how to rearrange my schedule to fit in an hour each day to train. I got a running diary, and read some inspirational books.

And I started running. A little each day. But when people asked me what I did, I never said, "I'm starting to run." I said, "I am a runner." Making the mental and emotional commitment made it hard to give up when things got tough.

My body changed. My muscles became hard and sleek. I found that I had more energy and stamina for the day. I had calluses on my feet, and even iced an injury or two. But more importantly, when I ran, I found a connection to my inner voice that I didn't know existed.

I always thought that the peace of running was in tuning out. The reality was that it allowed me to tune in. The focus and concentration on my pace, my gait, my breathing gave space for my thoughts to roam free. I couldn't waste the energy to constrain them. I found a focus.

After a few months I decided it was time to put some teeth in the game. I signed up for a 5K. I couldn't help but think about that old boyfriend and his derogatory remark. And here it was 15 years, two degrees, seven residences, two states, one husband and one child later. Could I pull it off?

I signed up for a small 5K benefit for the local high school track team. It was called the "Cherokee Chase." What I didn't know at the time is that the race got its name because it's about twenty-five members of the track team beating the pants off of twenty-five middle-aged folks (mostly their parents). When the gun went off and the race started I saw a blur where the front of the pack used to be. The person next to me whispered "holy—!" Or maybe it was me, I'm not quite sure. One thing I'm sure of, I was running.

After a half mile, I saw the hill. Now, I drive this path almost every day. I'm not exactly sure when the hill was installed and removed, but I swear that until that morning I'd never seen it before, and I'm sure I haven't seen it since. But it was there. And when I hit the hill, I thought I was toast. But I kept pushing.

I hit the first mile marker and the start of the field was already looping around to make their way to the finish line. Not exactly the motivation I was looking for, but reminded myself that I was doing this for me. And that I could do this, if I just held on.

My husband, son, and best friend had driven to the halfway point. They were cheering me on as I ran, pretty much alone at this point. My husband told me to keep going, looked at his stopwatch and yelled out to me something about my time. At this point, however, I was working on a mantra of "chugga chugga choo choo," which was unfortunately the last story I read to my son before we left for the race.

Although it seemed like forever at the time, now I can hardly remember the rest of the race. Except for the end. I came around the corner, somewhat unsure of where to go. I thought the end was at three different points, only to have people yell to keep running as I slowed my pace. Finally I finished. Alone. Second to last. But I finished.

That's when my husband brought me my official time. 30:32. My best time up until that point had been thirty-five minutes. I had accomplished more than I had hoped for. I told my son "Don't let anyone ever tell you that you can't do anything, because that is for you to decide."

My husband smiled. My best friend teared up. My son said "You smell skunky and need a shower." On the drive home, however, he told me he thought it was cool, and when he was six he was going to run the race with me, but he would run slower so I could keep up.

I told him not to be so sure since I have two more years to train. Who knows, by then I may be running marathons. After all, I am an athlete.

The truth of the matter is that I spent far more time running before I started running. Running from other people's expectations, running from my own, running from my fear of what I might do if I really committed to it.

So the next time I ate lunch with my friend, we were at the same restaurant, eating the same lunch.

"What *is* she running from?" she asked.

"Well, that's the funny thing about running," I said "You may start by running away from something at the beginning, but by the time you're halfway through, you find there's someplace that you're actually running to."

Forever Changed, Forever Runner

By Amy Abern

FALMOUTH, MASSACHUSETTS

I'm always amazed at the power of a single experience to completely change the course of one's life. A baby being born. Falling in love. Ben and Jerry's.

For me, one such experience came at the age of twenty-five after attending an Earth, Wind & Fire concert in Chicago. They ranked as one of my all-time favorite bands. When the band walked out on stage, I burst into tears. The people sitting next to me changed seats.

During the entire concert I remained overcome with emotion, watching them dance so gracefully to the songs I loved so much. Dance so gracefully. While singing. Huh.

Later that night, I decided that the members of band moved more on stage in one night than I had in several months. That bothered me. So I decided I would start running.

Mind you, there was no game plan in mind, any concrete motive or goal. The next day, I purchased a pair of cheap sneakers, laced up and took off. I ran an entire city block before almost passing out. The next day, I could barely walk. At the time, I was working as a waitress. I got a lot of sympathy tips that day.

The Amy pre-Earth, Wind & Fire concert would have thrown in the towel right then and used the sneakers as planters. But the Amy post-

Earth, Wind & Fire concert was more curious than anything else to find out what would happen if I kept running.

After a month, I made it through a mile. After two months, I could do two. At that point, I rewarded myself with real running shoes as my original sneakers self-destructed.

At three months, I added an exercise program to the three miles I ran every day, six days a week, including two hundred sit-ups, two hundred leg lifts and stretches that, attempted today, would result in traction. At four months from the first day I started running until three years later, I kept up a routine of running four miles a day six days a week along with the Stretching Regimen For Would-Be Contortionists.

While I hadn't taken up running to lose weight, I did. It wasn't my intention to lose three inches from my thighs and hips but it happened. Not that I was complaining.

Even greater than the physical benefits was the psychological. You've heard about people becoming addicted to running? It's not a fallacy. When you're done running, endorphins, natural pain-killing chemicals, are released into your system. They wash over you and it feels like all of your muscles are being coated internally with warm oil. Any physical tension dissolves in an internal massage of biochemical fingers. The result is a feeling of well-being, peace, and the joy of knowing you don't have to feel guilty if you decide to drink a chocolate malt later on.

My runs always ended at the beach. I enjoyed a delicious sensation of tingling cement in my legs. I found I could focus on nothing and stay with it—not drift into the land of "I should be's." I knew true peace and tranquility. When people say there's nothing like a runner's high, they're not lying.

With my new athletic prowess, I checked out other forms of exercise —swimming, aerobics, and weight lifting—and while they all had their benefits, none of them really did it for me the way running did.

At the age of twenty-eight, an accident effectively put an end to my first month of training for the Chicago Marathon. It was December and snow had turned to ice. I slipped and fell two miles into my run and broke off a piece of my ischium, a bone that connects the thigh to the buttock. The doctor told me I'd be able to run again, but I'd never be able to breakdance. After twenty minutes of grieving, I moved on.

Six weeks after my injury, I made my first attempt to get back on the running track. I lasted about a half a mile before the shooting pain in my leg turned into a shooting gallery. Discouraged, I drowned my sorrows in a hot fudge sundae.

A month later and a few pounds heavier, I went at it again, and the shooting gallery was a lot smaller this time. I made it through a mile and then after a couple of weeks, up to two.

The experience of living continued to sabotage all efforts to return fully my former endurance. At the age of thirty-three, I took a job in public relations, which meant I had to get up in the morning. As a waitress, I worked at night and slept late in the morning, eased into the day at my own pace and took my run in the early afternoon. Now I had to get up at the ungodly hour of 7:00 A. M. to sit at a desk all day.

I'd come home from work exhausted. My running went from six days a week down to two. The distance never went beyond two miles again. My thighs filled out. The peace I enjoyed right after a run still washed over me, but didn't last very long.

It would have been so easy to convince myself to quit. After all, I no longer fit into size seven jeans; my hips were expanding faster than the universe and since I wasn't running regularly, why bother at all?

The funny thing about transitions is how you never know that one has taken place until you're on the other side of it. At some point, running went from being a hobby to a part of my biology. I kept running simply because I wanted to.

For the next ten years, running served as a reward for finishing up a project, cleaning up the house or having enough energy and the time to expend it. No longer did I enjoy a regular running routine and as much as three weeks would go by without a run—but the option to run lived at the forefront of my conscience and was something always to be considered in the course of everyday living.

I'm forty-three now. Gravity is my second worst enemy, behind menopause. I am easily ten pounds overweight and those pounds aren't going anywhere.

I couldn't run four miles now if my life depended on it. But I can still run two miles, with a lot of stopping and starting up again. And I do those two miles when I can. Simply because I want to.

Sir John

Muhammad Shehzad Hanif

PUNJAB, PAKISTAN

Sitting in my armchair and just thinking of telling you my story certainly makes things difficult. Had I been on the track with my children (my trainees, my young fellows—I proudly speak of them as my children) I would be more comfortable, asking them to just concentrate, to measure their steps, to focus on what they are doing. In the meantime I'd be feeling a bit sluggish and one of my children would ask:

"Uncle Shan, why do you repeat so much?"

I'd be seated on the grass.

"What! Why do I repeat so much? Because you forget so much."

They'd laugh and we'd all be at ease. Another hectic session would be over.

I have come home but the whole day I have been thinking of what I would be say about me, about my career, my running, my sweet memories. I tried my best but Ramiz, my talented trainee whom I call my shining star, just did not let it go.

"Uncle Shan, you have to write it for me."

"My son! What's so special about me? I am just a physical trainer, an instructor who does not even know a handful of running. My son, I am not a writer."

"Uncle they just need a few words from you, from anyone who has got that special feeling about running. Please, Uncle Shan. I know it has been your passion. What else have you dreamt of? What else have you spent time on? You just go on. True feelings do not need words—they express themselves."

Ramiz stands steadfast and I find no way out.

It's recess time in the local orphanage. The kids are relaxing, playing and gossiping. The kids of the fourth grade are playing football. With six lads on each side they call it 'super-six'. The score is even at one each. Farhan makes an attempt but the ball crosses the sideline and drops just short of a kid.

"Hey you! Throw the ball back!" cries the goalkeeper.

"Would you let me play?" the kid asks.

"Hey, are you new here?" asks another kid.

Farhan snatches the ball saying, "How could you play with us? We're super-six and you can hardly kick the ball. Look at your legs. I think you cannot even walk with those legs." The kids laugh.

The bell rings, the kids go back to the classrooms but the new kid stays there.

He has forgotten that this is his first day. He has to go and attend the class. The only thing he remembers is: "I think you cannot even walk with those legs."

Suddenly he hears a soft voice, "Any problem my boy?"

He finds a man in a white uniform.

"Hey, my boy, why are you crying?"

The kid just bursts into tears and tells him the story.

"So my boy, what's wrong in it? You've really got thin and lean legs but even if you cannot walk, your legs could make you fly."

"Sir? You mean I can run?"

"You are in doubt? Do come to me after your class. I am Sir John," he says with a smile.

This was my first meeting with Sir John. I went to my class and in the late afternoon I went to see him in his room, but it was locked and a notice was near the keyhole, which read "My boy, I am waiting for you in the playground."

I was new in this orphanage. I had lost my parents in an accident when I was in third grade. Since then I was with my uncle but he was not ready to bear my expenses so he left me in this orphanage. I was lucky enough to meet Sir John and this marked the beginning of a whole new era for me.

I came out and asked a boy about the playground. He was going to the playground himself so I accompanied him to find Sir John standing in a corner with ten boys from different grades.

"Come, come my boy! Friends, let's have some introduction. So what's your name, my child?"

"Shan. Sir John."

"Wow. Shan Sir John. Isn't that interesting?" He laughed. "So boys, we'll start our exercise now, and Shan, for today you just see what they do."

I had never before seen such devotion. Sir John was so zealous in teaching us. I thought he was also a young lad like us, with so much enthusiasm, so much interest. He was there to explain everything. The way he taught us, it seemed so easy and the way he rectified our faults was gentle and clear. The main things he impressed upon us was concentration and self-confidence. He used to say, "My boys, do concentrate, rely on yourself, and the rest is all success, only success my children. Do remember, committing mistakes is forgivable but committing them again and again is not. If you learn from your mistakes, then success is always yours."

I did not disappoint the confidence that Sir John showed in me. My routine was different from my other fellows who made fun of it and said how silly I was to get up at five in the morning when even our hostel gatekeeper was asleep. I used to get up, take a bath, and rush to the sports ground where Sir John was already waiting.

"My boy, you are late again." Sir John would smile and we would start our training session. He was not a professional athlete but he wished I would be one some day. I learned very quickly the things he told me. Concentration and confidence were the master keys. He asked me never to lose heart from a defeat, not to mourn over it but get up and strive for another turn, for another attempt till another victory. We used to warm up and afterwards he asked me to run around.

I could not complete a whole round trip but he cheered me up and asked me to just stick to it to build steadiness. Sir John never cared about my speed, he only concentrated on my stamina and my mind-making. He wanted me to be a marathon runner. He used to say to me "My boy Shan, life is itself a marathon and how adventurous it feels to run a series of marathons in a long, life-long marathon."

I showed my intentions when I participated in the local community games that were held five months later. I won the first prize in the children's category. Sir John was so happy that day. When I passed my sixth grade, Sir John got permission from the principal, Sir Amir and I moved to his room. He took a great care of my diet, my sleeping hours and my study hours. It affected me directly and my health and fitness got a boost after it. My fellows, who used to laugh at me, now often asked me to join them in 'super-six'. Though I was not a soccer player, I played with them and it was my stamina and concentration that made me excel there too.

Time flew away with my childhood. Sir John had adopted me. I won race after race, moving to higher levels of competition. I was in twelfth grade and this was my last year in the orphanage. Sir John was not that quick now, but his vigor was the same. I was offered a scholarship from a training school of national repute because of my brilliant record. Sir John was really satisfied that I was on the right track now.

It was a whole new life there, a life full of thrills and competition, a life full of knowledge, and I got used to it soon. Sir John was not there with me but his letters were, his training and his remembered words were always there to help me. We were a group of seven who were being trained for the forthcoming national games. I was certain to represent my college. It was my nineteenth birthday that day when I found that I was selected to represent my college in the marathon run. My joy knew no bounds. The day I was packing up for my flight I called Sir John and told him about my nomination. He was feeling a bit feverish but he congratulated me at the top of his voice. I tried to inquire about his health but he said he was perfect. Later I found he was in terrible health but did not disclose it.

The day came in my life that I had dreamt of: my first appearance in a national competition. The way I had performed up till then, it was predicted that I'd be a winner by an easy margin. I do not know if I was overconfident or if I lost my concentration, but definitely it was not my day and things went wrong. I started it well and soon it was only me and another runner, someone who had lost to me earlier. It was the last half hour of the race when he began to press forward. I tried and tried, but it was too late. I still remember it was the last two minutes when I was so desperate that I forgot everything. I lost my balance and fell down. My ankle was hurt. I fainted on the spot. When I came to my senses it was all over.

Doctors told me that I would not be able to run for at least a year or so because my ankle was dislocated. I cried bitterly. My colleagues were there to support me with their encouraging words. I knew it was all over for my professional career. I looked for Sir John but did not find him. I asked about him but no one replied. I frantically asked again. Aslam passed an envelope to me. It was a letter from Sir John. I opened it.

"My child Shan! When you will read this, I will not be in this world. It seems that I cannot be there to congratulate you on your brilliant success . . ."

I could not read any more and fainted again. It took me a month to recover and I came back.

I have returned from the cemetery now and I visit the orphanage. I'm in the same old room where I've spent my whole life but it all appears to be unfamiliar without Sir John. I gaze at his photo on the wall.

"I lost it, Sir John. I could never win it. I have lost everything." Showing my walking stick, I speak to him tearfully.

"How could you, my boy?" I hear him saying. "It is a series of marathons, life-long, and you have just lost one."

The next day. The kids are having a break. I was just enjoying the sun when I heard two kids quarrelling.

"What's the matter, kids?" I approach them.

"You see he cannot play soccer but he insists on it."

"Why can't I?" asks the other kid, with his lean legs that hardly carry his weight.

His words came to me like a flash. It seemed as if Sir John was there. "How could you my boy? It is a series of marathons life-long and you have just lost one." It was all clear. I smiled.

"Hey kid, he's right, I think. But you want to play it really?"

"Yes."

"Do come to me after your class. By the way, my name is Shan. Uncle Shan."

There is a knock at the door. I open my eyes.

"Uncle Shan!" Ramiz knocks again. I heave a sigh and get off my chair to open the door.

The Trail

Kerry A. Gildea

ALEXANDRIA, VIRGINIA

With each heavy breath, each wisp of wind through my hair, each slap of my Nikes as they hit the black macadam of the trail, I thought I was running away. Further and further as I ran past each wooden mile marker, fallen leaves of brilliant yellow and orange, muddy brown and deep crimson crunched underfoot, breaking the silence.

Steadily I breezed though scattered streams of sunlight beaming through breaks in the trees. I was far away from the stress, crying, screaming, control, psychological warfare, guilt, and confusion of my failing marriage. My mind raced and my pace increased. Faster, faster, faster.

I wasn't running away at all. In fact, I was running to something. The trail did indeed take me to a place far away, somewhere I had never been before, a place of solace and strength, self-confidence, quiet endurance and inner peace. The trail led me to me.

"You can't run a marathon," he scoffed across the dinner table months earlier. "You aren't an athlete."

He had a point. I was not an athlete, not like he was. I did not look like an athlete. A few 10K races did not anoint me an athlete. I did not even look much like a runner—no cut muscles, no sinewy stature. I studied him. Towering over me at six-foot-two with his broad shoulders and long legs, he looked like an athlete. Star of his college basketball team. A high school highest score record never surpassed. I had seen all the pictures of his championship-winning foul shots, later hoisted on the

115

shoulders of his teammates. These were images of a younger, stronger, handsome, smart and funny man. I loved him . . . at one time. Now, always angry, he just scared me.

"But I want to try," I said. "I think you should at least let me try. If I get hurt, I promise, I will stop. I'll find a good training group. There are lots of them. My marathon book says with six months of progressively building mileage, even the beginning runner can . . . "

"No. You're no athlete." He slammed his hand on the table.

I was already defeated. If only I could convince him. A marathon would give me a chance to prove I was more than what I had become. Once assertive and full of life, I found myself shrinking down in my chair, feeling so weak and afraid, beaten down, compromised. I could see the anger grow in his eyes. My running was the least of our problems. I knew better than to continue the argument. For now.

"Even if you train, you will never do it," he said matter-of-factly, chomping on a piece of steak. "You'd never make it to the end."

We finished our dinner in silence, then he got up and walked away.

A week later I went to my first marathon training group run. He wasn't happy. But, I hadn't been happy for a long time. Preoccupied and allegedly working through every weekend, he would barely notice my Saturday morning absence. Secretly I registered for my first marathon. I would tell him little details. I would admit to running five miles when I ran seven, and seven when I ran fifteen. That approach bought me time. Maybe the 26.2 miles of a marathon was too far for the non-athlete. Perhaps I would fail. I needed to find out for myself.

I felt like I was running inside an oven. The Washington, D.C., humidity set in early and was far more brutal than in previous summers.

"Another code red day . . . a good day to be inside the air conditioning . . . don't leave your pets outside," the DJ warned as I swung my car into the parking lot before the seven A.M. run. Armed with energy bars and power gels, greased up with Vaseline and sun block, we took swigs from our water bottles and divided into pace groups. We were already sweating.

"Remember to take it slow, and drink your water," the group leader shouted to the crowd of some one hundred runners. "When you think you've had enough to drink, drink more and then drink again. If you get the chills it means that you are dehydrated and should stop. Remember to keep focused on completing the mileage. Slowly. Today's run brings us another step closer to our goal. We are going for twenty miles. Today the heat will make it feel like double that. Help each other, reach inside and go for it!"

Halfway into the run, my confidence nose-dived. It was too hot and too hard. I struggled to concentrate. Climbing the steepest hill, I heard his voice. "You'll never finish."

But the trail was full of angels with voices much louder than his.

There was Suzy, a.k.a. "Nature Girl," who named every species of bird and shared her killer recipe for mango margaritas. She never hesitated to double back for me when I lagged behind. And Missy, a seasoned marathoner who worked on Capitol Hill, got my mind off the pain by luring me into a political debate. True friends, they stood by me as I threw up after discovering that eating an orange slice at mile sixteen was not the best idea. J. R. had the corniest jokes and the kindest heart. Tom, faster than all of us, never passed a fellow runner without a high five.

The trail became the forum for our discussions, covering a lot ground from current events to first loves, career aspirations and worst fears. We appreciated side-by-side silence after mile seventeen. That summer I found respect and friendship, a lot of laughter and a desire to learn how far I could push my limits.

The marathon alumni made us first-timers their projects. Failing?

There was no failing, according to them. No nonsense about not making it to the end. They taught us to reach inside, way deep down to a place never tapped before. They convinced us we would cross that finish line. Failing, they said, was not an option. Their definition of an athlete was anyone with the courage to try.

Moments after our last and longest training run, I shoved a piece of watermelon in my mouth and we all laughed hysterically as the juice dripped all over my face. We could barely move. There was a break in the weather, with fall setting in. Twenty-two miles felt wonderful. We lumbered to our cars, gave each other sweaty hugs and slapped high fives. We were almost there. We were ready for 26.2.

Five months of training had passed and the marathon drew near. Maybe he had come around. He seemed to smile as I pulled my sweaty cap off my mass of messed-up hair and inched in the doorway following one of the toughest runs.

"Well, you're stubborn," he said. His half-smile suggested he was warming up to the idea. Surely he noticed my transforming body, the definition in my calves and newly sculptured arms, my waist trimmer than ever. Maybe he would find me attractive again. I felt attractive. I felt a fire inside. This must be what it felt like to be an athlete. I was happy. I didn't want to pick a fight. I wanted his approval.

"I can't believe I ran twenty-two miles," I beamed. "Can you believe it? I really think I am going to do this. And, I feel okay, really okay."

As he moved toward me, for a split second I thought he was going to hug me. Then he reached around, brushed his hand on my backside and said, "You would think you would lose some of this with all that running."

I lost my breath. Not seventeen miles, not twenty-two miles, not the intense humidity, blisters, or excruciating muscle cramps—nothing prepared me for that. I couldn't speak. I turned and lifted my lead-like legs up the stairs. I would not be defeated. Not now.

The cool shower gently drenched my head, washing the salt from my sunburned face. I held my head and the tears streamed down. He would not hear me in the shower. I would not share my pain. I vowed never to allow him to see me weak again. Not ever again. The fire inside overtook me.

I will never forget crossing the finish in the pouring rain. After all those humid runs, it was freezing and raining in torrents on marathon day. I was never colder, but never prouder. Never more alone, and never more content. There were painful moments and others filled with giddy excitement and raucous laughter. My inner athlete emerged. Yet, many of us ran alone that day. Not everyone had a partner or family or friends who understood. Some were lucky, like the couple who crossed the finish together. I envied what they had. Perhaps someday. With six months of intense training and 26.2 miles under my belt, I started to believe anything could be possible.

It's now four years and three marathons later. I am on the trail again. My pace is steady and my breathing is controlled. I am moving forward, gliding though each mile. The trail is welcoming and full of sunlight. The warmth of the fall day embraces me.

I don't hear his voice anymore. I am starting to forget his face. I am rarely sad or angry anymore. I am grateful for the trail and the angels that come with it. They have erased my tears. The trail took me on a journey I never anticipated when I started running. It led me to me, an athlete with courage and the will to try, to move forward, take control of life and make change. I am still learning, still running, faster and faster, farther and farther, mile by mile.

Going to the Chapel

Jennifer Rucinski

HARRISONBURG, VIRGINIA

I am a very, very slow runner. This is not a quality I enjoy or admire about myself, yet there it is. It is a fact that I have come to accept about myself, along with many others too uninteresting to anyone but perhaps my mother to care, but I am slow. Accepting this part of myself seems to be one of the great benefits of getting older if not faster; a sense of coming to peace with certain truths of my nature that are as firmly planted in me as roots to a tree. I am slow.

It hurt a bit to realize that Oprah ran a faster mile than I do; that my dogs still have energy to spare after a run with me. None of these realizations though have made me question why I continue to run. I crave running. I crave that sense of solitude, of inwardness that I am able to achieve only it seems while running. Clarity of thought and peacefulness of spirit are mine for just a thirty-minute investment.

No one would have ever mistaken me for an athlete in high school. I despised gym class, although I feel certain most girls of sixteen did and still do. I resented having to sweat after spending two labor-intensive hours preparing for my day. It was too unfair. The entire effort spent blow-drying my hair and perfecting my coordinating eye shadow would be shot with one field hockey game. Besides, the girls that were into sports scared me. I'd thought once to try out for the new girl's lacrosse team the school was forming, but after seeing some of the competition, I decided that taking up smoking was probably more my speed. I liked my teeth right where they were and as for my lungs, well, no one could see those.

College really wasn't much better. I was absolutely flabbergasted to realize that even there, at an institution of higher learning, I had a P.E. requirement. Certainly this could not be necessary to my major, that being art. In all honesty though, I felt pretty much the same way about all the classes I didn't want to take, like oceanography. I muddled through with a gymnastics class and was a bit offended when I only got a C, but at least the tumbling and twisting were over. I ended up with a D in oceanography but it was still passing so I counted myself lucky and moved on.

Over the years I waited tables and worked in retail, cursing my art degree repeatedly. Physically I was lucky to be thin enough without having to try too hard and I preferred to starve myself to get thinner rather than contemplate exercise in any form. On a few short attempts at fitness I would venture out for a run. After hearing one runner extol the beauty and virtues of running in the rain I tried it out for myself thinking that my life needed more beauty and virtue. One twisted ankle later I swore off running and swore off the friend who recommended it. Thus endeth my running career. Or so I thought.

While waiting tables at one of the local town hangouts I struck up a conversation with a man who owned a small landscaping firm. I'd recently started dabbling in flower gardening, although I knew absolutely nothing about horticulture. I thought that with this fledgling new hobby and my art background I might be onto something with landscape design. Amazingly he hired me. My first three weeks of work were pure hell. I thought for sure I was going to die from exhaustion. I was hauling dirt and digging holes and running rototillers. I had never even mowed a lawn. Through sheer willpower, not strength, I continued. Somehow as the days wore on I took a strange, sick pleasure in being that physically tired. I felt empowered by this new feeling, yet was entirely too drained to be able to do much with it.

Six years have passed since then and I am indeed a landscape designer. I rarely wear much makeup these days unless I feel inspired and the concept of "doing" my hair is putting it up in a ponytail. I still work on job sites but not nearly as much as I used to. I am thankful for that, believe me but I found something missing when I wasn't physically working like I had been. I'd go for a run every now and then thinking that I might gain weight if I wasn't laboring outside as often, but running was a habit that just wouldn't stick. Then I got engaged.

I am not sure of the chain of events that actually lead me to crave running. I feel certain it must have started in vanity since not only did I have my own impending wedding to prepare for, but was also preparing to be a bridesmaid in my brother's wedding. The latter prospect was much more terrifying, as my brother's intended insisted that the dresses we pick out include butt cleavage—yes, butt cleavage. Thankfully calmer heads and less than perfect butts prevailed and we all got to wear what we wanted as long as it was red—her other stipulation. That one I could live with.

So off I would go on a twenty or so minute jog, dutifully plodding along thinking that if I could just make it around this next corner I would let myself stop. The corner would come and go and before I knew it it was all over. Just like getting a shot at the doctor's office, the buildup was worse than the actual event. Slowly, imperceptibly I began to increase the time I spent on these runs. Then I decided to get in my car and see just how far I was running. Certainly I was up to three or four miles since it sometimes took me forty-five minutes or so to complete this death march. Hmmm . . . 2.3 miles. Really? Was it possible to move that slowly? Apparently it was.

I was crestfallen, but the time had come and gone for me to quit. It was too late. I was hooked. The solitude and the sense of accomplishment at the end of my run were too addictive. I started looking for ways to increase my speed, my endurance. I started to take notice of the foods I was eating and for the first time in my life considered food not the enemy it always had been, but the fuel that would enable me to become a better runner. I had entered the ranks. I was a runner, a bona fide athlete now. I could talk to other athletes about miles and stretches and carbs and feel pride in my body's ability to move without stopping for forty to fifty uninterrupted minutes. Never in my entire life had I been aware of the capabilities my body possessed for grace and strength and movement. I went running on my vacations. I went running on my honeymoon. If I went more than three days without a run I started to feel disjointed. How this happened is still a mystery to me. I never will know what turned running into a welcome habit versus a loathsome chore but I am thankful.

I am thankful to have stumbled upon something that I truly believe will be my fountain of youth. I am in better shape now, physically, mentally, and emotionally than I ever could have imagined myself to be. I have no desire to run a marathon, considering that at this point it would take, say, a day and a half to finish, but I'm keeping my options open. I never thought I would get married either, or see the three mile mark, but both have happened so I've also come to realize: you just never know.

I have heard it said that life is what happens to you while you are waiting for it to begin. Running gives me the chance to catch up to my life; to fully be present in every aspect of what is going on inside of me and around me. It allows my thoughts to filter through my head as they will, my body the chance to prove what it can do and my spirit the necessary reflection to realize that I am an athlete after all. It just took the impending threat of a wedding dress and some butt cleavage to prove it.

A Runner's El Dorado

Joe Crisp

VICTORIA, TEXAS

Slowly, slowly it sinks in. I'm plodding along state highway 185 toward Bloomington at 6:30 on New Year's morning. Every step drives it home. What am I doing here, on this day, at this hour? I'm here because running has changed my life.

Bloomington is a small town near Victoria, Texas, where I live. Most of the eighteen hundred folks who live there work in Victoria, or at one of the nearby petrochemical plants. As a haven from city taxes, Bloomington lacks some amenities, but it does boast a Dairy Queen, a high school, a few churches, and a convenience store that fills the needs of fishermen headed for the coast.

I've decided to run to Bloomington because, at twelve miles from Victoria, it's a stretch for me. For years, I had never run more than six miles. I figured folks who ran marathons were aliens in human-like bodies with bionic capabilities. But lately, a friend has been egging me on to try a marathon, and I've run first eight, then ten miles. I figure Bloomington is a good chance to explore the higher ranges of mileage. I pick New Year's Day because the weather is cool and I like to celebrate holidays with special runs.

I don't know how long it will take me to run to Bloomington, but I figure a couple of hours ought to do it. As I creep out of the house in the predawn darkness, I ask my sleepy wife to pick me up at the Bloomington store at eight.

I've already run three miles or so by the time I hit the city limit and head southeast toward Bloomington. At this hour, and on this day, there's not much traffic. I take the left side of the four-lane, divided road. The sun has come up on a chilly, overcast day, with a gray sky hanging like a curtain.

Shortly after leaving town, I pass the old Welder Ranch. The red-brick, Spanish-style house hides mysteriously in a grove of live oaks. The trees sprout like an island from the wide, grassy plain on which graze the cattle that, in an earlier time, sustained the local economy. The house is set far back from the road, as if deliberately distancing itself from the fast pace of the highway.

A couple of miles later, I pass a newer symbol of south Texas. The Dupont chemical plant rises in the distance on my right, its fantastic maze of pipes and cylinders puffing out billows of steam that linger in the chilly air. I've passed both the ranch and the plant many times by car, but only today, at the slower pace of a run, does it occur to me how I've symbolically bridged two eras of local history. These two landmarks, so different in appearance, have something to do with each other. They've both brought wealth and settlers to town.

Another two miles, and I'm passing through Crescent Valley. Crescent Valley is not so much a town as a place, occupied by a few houses and the Crescent Valley Baptist Church. Its idyllic name comes from a slight undulation in the coastal plain that passes for a hill. Driving, one scarcely notices the slope, but now, having run seven or eight miles, I find myself climbing a mountain of monumental proportions.

I'm approaching ten miles now, pushing my upper limit. I'm still surprisingly strong. I see a sign that says, BLOOMINGTON 3. In the distance, the town's water tower rises above the plain like a lighthouse, guiding me into port. I quicken my pace, lengthen my stride.

The city limit sign looms on the right: BLOOMINGTON. I'm pounding along the town's main street. The Dairy Queen, with its red teardrop sign, flies by on the left. Two blocks ahead, I see the flashing red of the town's only stoplight. On that corner stands the convenience store.

And now I've done it. I slow to a walk in the parking lot. My gray sweatshirt is soaked, in spite of the morning chill. Sweaty and disheveled, I enter the store. The clerk eyes me as I skip the cold drinks and head straight for the bathroom.

A few minutes later my wife arrives. I settle into the front seat beside her, enjoying that delicious, tired feeling that comes after a run. We check the odometer on the way back. It hits exactly fourteen miles as we turn into the driveway at home.

I've begun the year with the longest run of my life. This run is the confidence builder I need for the marathon. I've run over half the distance, and I'm not half-dead. I figure now I can make the full marathon—and I do, four times over the next five years.

But the marathon did not change my life. I've set goals and achieved them before. The marathon was a goal different in kind, but not in quality, from others. A far more fundamental lesson was learned on New Year's Day, 1991.

It comes to me every time I drive that stretch of 185. As I pass the landmarks—the ranch, the plant, the hill—I remember how I saw them differently that day, saw so much more than I had ever seen before. I glimpse the distant water tower, and the sleepy town that lies beneath it becomes the object of an epic quest, a sort of runner's El Dorado.

I found much more than Bloomington at the end of that run. To see the extraordinary in the ordinary is a gift I doubt I'd have without running.

One Block at a Time

Lori A. Dinkins

MINNEAPOLIS, MINNESOTA

I loathe running and my life is better for it. The shoes are fabulous; the outfits, adorable; the effervescent glow, inspiring; the heavy yet methodical breathing, simply orgasmic. But the act of running does not agree with me and yet I am fascinated by the idea of becoming a runner. For years I watched, admired and occasionally followed (in my car) runners doing their thing. On them, running looks graceful, peaceful, and somehow spiritual. When I run the earth literally wobbles beneath me.

A few years ago, I decided to take up running as my new form of exercise. I had been a sporadic walker for years and thought I should graduate to a higher form of movement. I read magazine articles instructing me how to prepare for my first run. I purchased the appropriate clothing, promising to allow my body to breathe. I drank the recommended amount of liquids, relying on my body to retain its usual amount of water for hydration during the run.

On one gloriously crisp Saturday morning, I decided to pop out of bed and go for a run. Ironically, every other runner in the neighborhood shared this thought. As I performed the stretches I remembered seeing Oprah do before she ran the Chicago Marathon, I saw swarms of people buzzing by wearing their colorful running shoes and sparkling smiles. I jumped up and down in my new colorful shoes, running in place a couple of times like I'd seen my neighbors do before their run. I took two puffs of my asthma inhaler and eagerly ran down the street, joining the rest of the athletes. I wasn't sure how fast or slow I should be going, so I decided stepping twice in each box on the sidewalk was fast enough. I felt so light as I ran down the sidewalk; I glanced down at my feet to make sure they were touching the ground. And sure enough my feet were connecting with the pavement falling in step to the rhythm of my running self. My body was orchestrating a musical piece I did not recognize, pulsing and beating and throbbing and burning.

By the time I reached the third block I was huffing and puffing and sweating my retained water. My shorts seemed to be a size smaller than they were when I put them on. My walking muscles refused to participate in my new choice in exercise. My breasts choreographed a dance called the *wiggle and jiggle*, and my lungs demanded a third and fourth puff from my inhaler. I was confused and a bit disoriented. I stopped abruptly, turned around and scanned the topography of the previous three blocks hoping to find I had just climbed a steep hill, which would be an obvious answer to my bewilderment. Instead I discovered a flat terrain with a slight downhill slope. I put my hands on my knees, hoping this position would allow more air to enter my lungs. I thoroughly scanned my body hoping to find ten-pound weights secretly strapped to my ankles. Instead of weights, I was shocked at what I discovered. Fat. An abundance of fat. A plethora of cells containing an inordinate amount of fat. I was discovering my body for the first time in the middle of this gloriously crisp Saturday morning in the presence of my fellow runners. My inner thighs were chaffed because my shorts had run for cover finding refuge in my crotch; the fat-flap of my lower belly—which I fondly refer to as Junior—seemed to have invited friends over without my knowledge; and my face was so swollen I must have looked like I was storing nuts in my cheeks for the winter. It was at this moment I realize I was overweight. Not a breaking news story for most passersby, but a true awakening to the one with the best seat in the house.

As I shamefully turned around to walk back home, a van full of teenage kids drove by, one of them leaning his head out of the window calling to me, "Hey lady, you have a wedgie!" Laughter. Defeat. Motivation.

My tale does not end with a Richard Simmons's success story. It does not end with before and after pictures of my puckered body. And unfortunately, it doesn't end with me chasing after that van and sitting on the obnoxious kid. However, my humiliating and fortunately humbling experience turned me into an inspired runner wannabe. On that day of truth, I ran three blocks before I nearly collapsed and since then I have doubled the number of blocks I run before my knees buckle.

I used to admire from a distance the steep-incline-treadmill runner, respect from afar the everyday-after-work runner, and be secretly in awe of the regardless-of-the-weather-outdoor runner. Today, I am a combination of those runners, six blocks at a time.

The crushing reality of the strength, endurance, and stamina required of runners nearly sent me back to the walking minor league. But the simple possibility of running one mile without stopping is worth the dreadfully gratifying trek down my neighborhood street. The days of sitting on my porch watching others participate in life are over.

The Run

C. A. Robert

KISSIMMEE, FLORIDA

In my early years I often wondered why my parents bothered to name me. As the youngest of four, in a small close-knit community, I was known, for the most part, only as the "kid sister." The fact that very few people actually knew or even cared what my real name was didn't bother me. In fact it sometimes worked on my behalf.

When I started kindergarten my teacher turned out to be a big fan of my brother Steve. Even though it had been many years since he was a student of hers, she was happy enough to have his little sister in her class.

I entered the first grade with a teacher who was new to the school. For the first time I was on my own with no past to shadow or shield me. Before I even had a chance to decide if I liked this new status or not we were marched single file to the school's gymnasium. After being introduced to our gym instructor, our teacher left. And with her my individuality.

Having a last name that begins with W, you get used to being at the end unless you happen to have a Zimmerman or Yeats in your class. So, I was surprised when the instructor, who was consulting her list of names suddenly called out mine first.

"Warpell?"

"Here." I answered.

"Are you related to Vicki Warpell?"

Warpell isn't what I would call a common name. As far as I knew all

Warpells were related. "She's my sister."

I swear to this day, her eyes brightened. I should have felt pride as my fellow classmates patiently listened to how well Vicki could throw a ball and how high she could jump. I should have at least felt that I had an "in," but instead I felt a sense of dread starting to form in my stomach. Somehow I knew this time there would be no free ride on a family member's coattails.

It didn't take too many gym classes to prove that though I had been passed the torch, I had not only stumbled, but extinguished it for good. I never actually failed gym class, but you could tell by the look in her eyes that I had failed her. To give her credit she held out hope for the longest time. As though I might suddenly show up in the gymnasium empowered with some long dormant athletic ability. By the end of fifth grade she had finally let it go.

On that last day of school we had a "Be Fit" day. I think the faculty decided that hundreds of grade schoolers, anxious for summer break to begin, would wreak less havoc if occupied out of doors. They set up hurdles, high jumps and a makeshift track for running. None of which was available in our small gymnasium.

My class was due up next for the race. The thought of being able to run at school, after all those years of being told not to, might have actually excited me, except for the fact that I was too busy drowning in my own self-pity.

I, along with my mom and dad, would be moving the following week to another town. My older siblings, by this time, had all spread their wings and were out on their own. There was no need for the three of us to stay in a four bedroom home. Even if it was all I had ever known.

I was prodded by the toe of my friend's sneaker to get moving and take my place in line. I got up from my grassy seat dragging my depression along with me. Looking at the long stretch of track before me I felt some trepidation creeping in. When had I ever run? Sure, around my small yard. And down the street but I always had to stop at the corner to look both ways before continuing on. This was too far. I was never going to make it. I would leave this school and this town with the memory of me gasping as I walked to the finish.

Someone shouted, "Go," and I was off. I had always been one of the smallest in my class, but for some strange reason I felt bigger, taller. I didn't think. I just stretched out one leg in front of the other. Somehow I had managed to break free from the pack in the first few yards. From there out it was clear sailing and that is exactly what I did that miraculous afternoon. I sailed all the way to the finish and felt like I could keep on going—forever.

I didn't know or care if the gym instructor had witnessed my triumph or the ribbon I received. I did take it home and pin it on my wall. I told my family that I had participated in a race, but left it at that. If I'd told them that I had won they would have been proud and congratulated me, but it was something I wanted to hug to myself.

That night I wondered how many times Vicki had felt this way, then felt a stab of pity that the answer was probably never. This was a once in a lifetime high. The feelings of euphoria had by now washed away, but they had left in their place a new found sense of confidence.

Maybe moving wouldn't be so bad. A chance to be known firsthand for me and me alone. Besides, high school wasn't too many years off and my brother, Mark, had set quite a few swim records that had yet to be broken. It wouldn't be bad starting a new life, my own.

That was over thirty years ago. Since then I have run many times, though not in competitions or races. Instead my runs have been through the fields behind the new home my parents and I moved to or more recently, chasing after and playing numerous games of tag with my children. All special and all memories that I will forever cherish. My first run though, will always be my best.

Grace Asked Me To Dance

Jane McDermott

OAKLAND, CALIFORNIA

To start, my reasons were rote: thirtieth birthday, just quit smoking, time on my hands. I would use my enhanced lung capacity to thwart the ravages of my advancing years—that's what I would do! I would avoid going anywhere where there was smoking, which was just about anywhere I would go. I would—run. Today, I am not sure if it was about running or about fleeing. In fact, with no clue as to what a life without cigarettes might look like, I was attempting to invent one. I was inventing a nonsmoking life the way someone who had never seen cat might draw one—based purely on imagination and secondhand description.

I decided to run because I liked the word "athlete" and because of an image I held of myself as a physical person. In truth, I had avoided all activity that could not be done while smoking. I was about as physical as kelp. I decided to run because I thought, *"how hard can it be?"* I did hold a jot of a memory of how much I had loved to run when I was a child, of how I would imagine myself to be a wild horse running free, of how I would just run myself right out of the life I lived and into a better one.

Perhaps in that place where thought begins, I germinated that memory into a lump of clay that I threw onto the wheel, trying to center and shape it into a recognizable vessel. I could be that horse; I could find that life. Little did I realize that what I was really seeking is the difference between conquering and surrendering. To find this difference would require stripping bare a lot of fancy ideas I had about devotion and discipline. There is nothing you can read that will teach you a thing about either of these two words.

Of course, I would not be a runner by imagination alone. There would be a few tolls.

There is a kind of pain that comes with new running that is like no other I have ever experienced. It's a pain that runs down into the marrow of your bones. You can be no other thing but the pain in those beginning days of running. There is an exquisite self-knowledge that comes with it, a blessing and curse to we who have worked so hard to know nothing about ourselves. In the beginning, pain transmits messages through your body that you have been too numb to feel and are now ill prepared to receive. Deep, deep, deep. It is impossible to deny, much less ignore your inner process with pain like this.

Because you are ignorant and don't know any better (you used to *smoke*, remember?) you keep running. It hurts so much to run. Climbing stairs is such torture that you are ready to confess to just about anything. And you do start to confess things. Things that you have forgotten about for years come bubbling to the surface and you admit to them like a war criminal. You are aware that this deep, inner pain is *following you around*. So you keep running. The pain now is chasing you, but, after those first dozen or so tender miles, it drops back.

So now what do you do? You run more. You run farther. All these crimes and sins—whatever they are—run with you. And guess what? They're not so bad. They'll never be your best friends, but you at least have some vague sense that they have something to give you rather than take away.

You can run like this for a long time, years and years. I did. You can also go to one more place. I did that, too.

When you attempt longer and longer distances another demon

appears—fear. Fear comes in many flavors. I've tasted several of them. The fear of not being able to get back from the place you're heading— wherever that is. The fear that you will not have what it takes. The fear that you are not worthy of the challenge. The fear that you will be discovered for the fraud you really think you are. No guts. No moral fiber. A mere husk of a human being. Far greater than the trauma anyone can inflict upon you are those we deliver to ourselves.

What happens then? You deal with the fear the same way you dealt with the pain—first, by trying to outrun it, then by cloaking yourself in it. Ah yes, that conquering versus surrendering notion—here it is again.

Chattering like a squirrel you enter the fear, soak in it, then come to wear it and allow the fear to inform you, in fact, to protect you—there are many real things to be afraid of in long distance running. Fear is actually an ally. It can keep you from doing something stupid and injuring yourself. But in order for that to happen, you have to explore the various strata of fear, separating them one from the other. Good, inform- ing, protecting fear in the "keep" pile. Bad, toxic, debilitating fear in the "discard."

Step by step, you place some distance in front of the place where you started. And what do you learn from this? You are both source of and solution to your own suffering. You create distress in your life and with grace you find the means for relief. Over time, you do get stronger. You go on. Remember that you are not running on the ground, but over it. Like it or not, you are part of this alive world. Life is fleeting; try to keep up—run if you have to.

What else? Just this—running has allowed me to bear witness to the divine within myself. For when it is right and I am removed from thought, it is to know that in that moment I am one with all living things, sharing this breath. I belong here and am in good company. For a crystal instant I know that I am running in the company of angels and the course that I'm running lies in the palm of God's hand.

Would I have come to touch this place some other way? Perhaps. But this is the way that grace has found for me. Briefly now, I can be that wild horse I imagined in my youth.

I've run three marathons now. The last quite recently so the cadence of the day is still fresh in my mind. Thump, thump, thump. The pounding of the pavement, the beating of my heart. It's hard to get there so that you can appreciate how simple it is when you arrive.

Who knew?

Life Is Too Short

Kami Holt

OVERLAND PARK, KANSAS

Wanderlust was what drove me to complete most of my college classes outside of the usual university setting. I studied in Hawaii for my first year, followed by my sophomore year in Europe, where I spent four months in London and two months in Italy. A six-month study abroad in Jerusalem topped off my third year of school. Upon returning home, I dreamt of a career surrounded by natural beauty, world affairs, and exotic cultures (just like my travels), and found the perfect fit with a major in geography. After graduating from BYU with a Master's degree, I was elated when I was hired to teach geography classes starting the fall semester that my husband, Gary, and I arrived in Baltimore. Gary had been accepted to study dentistry at the University of Maryland for the next four years, and I was happy to have a teaching job lined up in our new city. However, after much discussion about job stability and salary (I would make very little as an adjunct professor), we made the agonizing decision that I would put teaching on hold, turn down the job offer, and work as a secretary to make more money and have more job security while he attended dental school.

As a secretary I felt like a fish out of water. I was in the wrong place. I didn't care about my work; I was trained to do something else, something that I loved. I was overqualified and under-appreciated, and ended up quitting job after job, ultimately going through three secretary jobs in two and a half years. Even as a student, I didn't sit inactive in front of a computer as much as I did as a secretary. Moreover, Gary was so involved in his studies early on, that I rarely saw him; I felt single again. To be active, I did aerobics in our tiny, 450-square-foot highrise apartment six days a week, but despite that, the weight piled on. Here I was in a brand new city, working jobs I detested, rarely seeing my husband, and getting pudgier by the day. I was very unhappy and confused, but things were about to change.

Early one winter morning, a massive eight-alarm fire started on the fifteenth floor of our thirty-story building. We were very lucky to have gotten out of the building, and to have had minimal damage to our belongings on the fourteenth floor. We were, however, relocated to another property out of the city because our apartment was condemned due to smoke and water damage. Immediately, we packed our belongings, rented a U-Haul and found our new home in the suburbs of Baltimore. Many of our friends who lived on the floors above us were not as lucky, losing literally everything to the fire. Some were students just like Gary, who had to decide whether or not to stay in school, or to go home to their parents to recuperate. Additionally, an older woman lost her life trying to get down the stairwell through the smoke and heat of the fire.

The fire shocked me into realizing that life is too short to be unhappy, too short to put off your dreams, too short to be unhealthy. After moving to the suburbs I found myself spending more and more time outdoors, away from the concrete jungle of inner-city Baltimore, just thinking about my life. I began walking on the neighborhood high-school track. Wanting to go faster, I tired of walking and attempted to run. This wasn't very easy, you see, I had never run more than a mile before, and that was probably only once for a grade in gym class. I had always been a dancer in high school, and even college where I enrolled in upper-level ballroom, ballet, and tap dance classes just for fun. But I loved being outside in the cold air, and running just seemed to work. It didn't happen immediately, though. I celebrated and congratulated myself when I completed my first lap around the track. My smile was so big, you'd think I had won the lottery. The next milestone was a mile—four continuous laps!—and mission accomplished. I remember jumping up and down after I ran three miles in a row. What freedom! What exhilaration! What accomplishment! Running was very difficult for my body to learn to do; I used to have to stretch for forty-five minutes after a thirty-minute run, but once I trained my leg muscles to run, it became easier. Practice, patience and persistence were necessary ingredients. Early spring was in the air, I was becoming healthier and happier than I had been in a long time, and I was beginning to have a positive outlook on life.

Running, I learned, makes one's thoughts flow smoothly and with clarity. I was able to think about things in great detail while going around and around the track. I found myself thinking that the time had come to again pursue my dream of teaching, no matter the drop in salary. So I quit my third and last secretary job and began applying for classes to teach that spring semester. It was a leap of faith to quit a stable job only hoping for another one so quickly. But luckily, adjunct teaching positions are not too difficult to come by and oftentimes the departments that are hiring are just as relieved to find a qualified instructor, as the instructor is to find a class. I was offered three classes at three different colleges, and began teaching as a new full time job. Teaching was fabulous; it was challenging; it was satisfying; it was frightening. Just like running was.

My life continued changing into that summer and fall as Gary's curriculum eased up and I saw more of him. A non-runner also, he became interested in running after seeing the changes in me, and together we set a goal to run a marathon. We trained through that winter (my favorite time to run), and ran the Baltimore-Annapolis marathon that March. I was elated with a 4:18, but Gary blew me out of the water running a sub-3 hour first marathon in 2:58! Racing a marathon distance seemed like the natural next step in our running lives. It wasn't the "culmination" of our first year of running, it was just the beginning of a life filled with it! For me, there was no pressure to go fast, there was little fear of not finishing, and I knew I would continue running after it was done. Two days after the marathon, it was nice to be back on the streets, with no training mileage requirement, just running to run. The race was a great accomplishment for both of us, and we're looking forward to Gary's Boston debut.

I am in my seventh month of my first pregnancy, and running five times weekly. I run much slower now and with the added help of a pregnancy belt, but that doesn't bother me at all as long as I keep running. It makes me free—free from the backaches of pregnancy, and free from the extra weight gain as a result of my ravenous appetite. I also feel that it has beneficial effects on my unborn baby, throwing extra oxygen and blood flow her way. The next step in my running life is a goal of a post-baby marathon next fall, and I can't wait to make it happen. I enjoy the feeling of running slowly and smoothly, with the camaraderie of other runners. But mostly, I love that feeling after it's over.

How has running changed my life? It inspired me to quit dead-end jobs, and fulfill my dream of teaching geography. It gave me back my healthy, fit body and returned to me my self-esteem. It gave me a new outlook on life, and reaffirmed the importance of being happy every day. It re-introduced to me the beautiful, invigorating outdoors. Also, running is an activity that my husband and I can enjoy together, as a family.

And you'd better believe I'm shopping around for a great running stroller for runs with our new baby.

Those early days in Baltimore seem like a distant, strange memory. I like to remember, instead, the day I began running and the life changes that followed.

How I Learned To Stop Worrying and Love Running

David Barber

SANTA CLARA, CALIFORNIA

The biggest change in my life wrought by running has been the sense of superiority and grandiosity I gain from knowing that I have run to the best of my ability for the distance of my choosing. I have been transformed from a meek, mild 98-pound Nowhere Man to a swift, sleek Walter Mitty.

I started running seriously out of concerns for health and weight. These are admirable reasons to start running, but not reasons that lend themselves to a prolonged stay in the runner's world.

I needed to find a reason to continue running after the initial resolutions about health and weight had been fulfilled. I have to admit it was hard at first to find a characteristic of running that appealed to me. It was agonizing, hot, and sweaty and just generally damn hard work. I kept asking myself, why would anyone want to subject himself to this? Why am I subjecting myself to this? Who but the Marquis de Sade could possibly gain any pleasure from plantar fascitis and Ilio-Tibial Band Syndrome? But then I discovered the sense of satisfaction (read moral superiority) after finishing a long hard run. Wow!

I am a great elitist snob and always have been. So without a doubt, this inner feeling of self-worth provided as a consequence of pounding the pavement in a rapid repetitive manner has probably been my greatest discovery and has been what has kept me at it for so long. I see another runner and my first thought is "I am good, I can take him!"

It took running to awaken the Frankenstein's monster sleeping deep in my soul (it was probably jarred awake from all the pounding on the pavement). I am no Steve Prefontaine. I could, with some training and a stiff tailwind, probably break a six-minute mile. But in my mind I can be as fast as the wind. Finishing the last stretch of a 10K, I am Roger Bannister running the first sub-four mile. It isn't my actual talent that gives me such morally superior pleasure, but my imagined talent.

I feel affection for fellow runners, but as in everything, there is a class system (we all need somebody to look down on). At the top are your elite runners (mostly Kenyan) who can do marathons in my best 10K time, followed by the fair-to-middlings and other lesser peoples. I fall somewhere in the middle. But what sets me apart from the other middle-of-the-packers is my firm belief, in my head, that I am the greatest runner on the road at any given time. I was given the self-belief of Muhammad Ali. If I had been granted the natural talent given world class runners, I could have been a contender.

Which is not to say that I am disappointed in my lack of natural ability. No, I don't need to actually win an Olympic medal or anything to feel morally superior. I feel just great inside my head. It doesn't matter if I enter a race with any of a number of world class athletes because I know that I am the best. That's really all that matters.

World-class athletes can only go one place from world class and that's down. Even the mighty must fall. I, however, can never fall because I am always the best in my head. My pace may slow, and it may not be as easy as it once was to recover from a longer than usual run, but none of this matters because I am not physically the best, but mentally. Which, I think is even better. I don't have to worry about broken records or losing the world championship (and I don't have to wait four years). It's all in my head.

This doesn't mean that I don't respect world-class athletes. I do. The work they put in is astounding. Not to mention the mental anguish over constantly vying for the top slots (or failure to achieve one of the top slots. Being at the top is never easy. But, like I said, I am still the best because I say so in my head.

So, the reader may be thinking about now that all running has really achieved for me is changing me from a quaint if pudgy nice guy to a pretentious butthead with delusions of grandeur. This may be true. I am not as nice as I used to be and people look at me differently now than before (usually because of the faraway look on my face as I daydream about great races). Being the best, even just mentally, is tough work without a lot of time for pleasantries. There is a lot of pressure in being the best. But like I said, being at the top is never easy.

And I wouldn't have it any other way.

Everything I Need to Know I Learned from Cross-Country Running

Anne Thornton

BUCKHANNON, WEST VIRGINIA

I was a high school cross country runner—and my parents often asked me why. I was never the best runner on the team, though I may have accumulated the most injuries. I have had twisted ankles, torn Achilles, and asthma attacks. Running made me tired, and sometimes cranky. "Why do this to yourself? Give it up," my mother said. But I couldn't. Running is what relaxed me, helped me make my best friends, and taught me the most important lessons I could learn about life.

Running is a lot like life. First, there will almost always be those who are better than you are. In my running career, I soon learned I would always be behind two of my teammates—the Kleinhoffer twins. No matter how hard I tried, I just could not beat them. It used to really bother me, until I realized that I ran faster because I was chasing them. In life, we will meet people who are better at whatever we are trying to do. We can react by backing away and giving up, or by being challenged to work harder. The Kleinhoffers taught me to be glad for competition, not resentful of it. In fact, these competitors became two of my best friends.

On cross country courses, I learned there were always new ways to twist my ankle. If there was a hole on the course, I managed to find it and step in it. I think life is like that, too—there are lots of holes out there

151

waiting for us. There are times when we will make wrong moves and maybe get hurt. But the important thing to remember is that my twisted ankles healed, and I was able to run again.

Cross country required lots of training. No one succeeds in a race without putting in a lot of practice miles. Hills, dirt roads, pools, and the track were the scenery I saw in my life for four years. This training gave me lots of time to think and reflect about who I am and what I wanted to be. It also prepared me for the rigors of the actual meets.

Cross country also taught me to pace myself and learn to rest. Often I started a race too fast and by the second mile, I was in trouble. I think you should work hard in life, but take some time to rest. Slow down, take a few deep breaths. If you do, you will improve your odds of finishing whatever project you start.

Cross country always made me strive for my best. Every course was different and difficult, but when we ran a personal record, we received pins and sometimes milkshakes. (The milkshakes, I now realize, may have been counterproductive.) In cross country, I learned that while I could not outrun the Kleinhoffers, I could improve my own times. It taught me that I should strive to be better tomorrow than I was today.

Finally, cross country taught me how important support was from others. Hearing the cheers along the sidelines and being supported by coaches helped even on a bad day. I must admit I considered quitting cross country—like after the county meet when I had an asthma attack and could not finish the race. However, I kept showing up because of my parents', teammates', and coaches' support.

"Good Job!" or "Keep it up!" were words we often exchanged as a team during meets and workouts. It was so encouraging to hear someone cheer you on in the lonely stretches of running. In a meet, only the top five women score points. However, because of our bond, our sixth and seventh runners' accomplishments were never forgotten. We recognized them as much as our first place runner. Our team worked together and supported each other so well that we won the first girls' cross country league championship in my high school's history. I think life is a lot like that. Don't quit, even when you are tired and discouraged. Keeping trying, and things will get better.

The bond we had went beyond running; we were friends from the start. We ran, ate, talked, laughed, and hung out together for four years. If someone was down or needed to talk, we were all there for her. We became a unit that clicked because we knew each other so well. This was truly the best experience I ever had. It taught me leadership, communication, cooperation, but most importantly teamwork and friendship.

Since coming to college, running has become a way for me to relax and focus on my life. When school seems overwhelming, I go running. When I have had a great day, I go running. Although I am not running on a team, running is still a very vital part of me because of my high school cross county experience.

Eat My Dust

Kelly Leonardo

CHESTER, NEW YORK

A little weasel lives in the dark abyss of my mind. She waits patiently in the shadows, watching me struggle and sniffing the air for smoky wisps of fear and doubt to get high on. When she senses anything remotely resembling a personal growth moment, she darts out, grabs my jugular with her needle-sharp teeth and rushes back into her cold underground haven, dragging me and my limp resolve through the dirt. Dozens upon dozens of my skeletal and unfulfilled dreams lie in a dusty heap in the corner of my psyche—like bones picked clean and discarded.

What is it about the fear of pain that makes me run away from taking care of myself or from pushing at the safe boundaries of the tight little burrow I inhabit? I began asking myself this question because of something that seemed so small, but left me amazed that such an innocuous event could unleash so many emotional critters into my peaceful mental landscape.

It started when I complained to a friend recently that even with all of the working out I've done lately, I still can't get rid of the wrinkled layer of dachshund skin that ripples across my otherwise trim tummy. It's been there in ever-shrinking proportions for nine years now. I said that I thought this final, stubborn roll may be a permanent reminder of what gaining nearly sixty pounds on a diet of Haagen Dazs and burritos during pregnancy does to a body. I don't really worry about weight, but this skin thing annoys me. My friend rolled her eyes and told me—as if it was the most obvious and natural thing in the world—like telling someone who's thirsty to drink a glass of water—to "go running."

Hah! My best friend in high school ran for our cross-country team. Every day she limped to the cafeteria for lunch in some form of dull and aching or sharp and excruciating pain. I myself dreaded the occasional mandatory two-mile run around the outdoor track during gym class. I know for a fact that running hurts. The very thought of choosing to put my body through that kind of torture struck me as ludicrous.

My response, "Oh, no, I'm no runner. I'm not built for that," sounded even more ludicrous and more importantly, habitual and false. Where did that nay-saying voice come from? It sounded disturbingly like the voice of that weasel I first remember hearing when I was fourteen years old. After two years of ballet, the much-anticipated transition to toe shoes had occurred. While I had never been very good, ballet suddenly lost what little charm and grace I brought to it in the grips of my painfully laced and arched feet. How on earth had girls in China ever lived with having their feet bound every day? I made it through two classes, whining incessantly about the pain, oh dear God, the pain, then told the teacher, "I don't think I'm built for ballet, I think I'm too tall."

It was true, I'd probably never have danced for a living given my height, but that fear-mongering little weasel had taken over. Dance became a part of my past, forming instead, a foundation for that heap of old bones to which I would add so many other dreams over the years— things like relationships, my education, a writing career, modeling, and guitar lessons, just to name a few.

Let's be clear, running hurts. A lot. All over. But now, twenty years after the great ballet burial, the time has come for me to face my fear of pain and the challenging aspects of my life. So at the age of thirty-four, out of breath and fatigued most days just from the effort of standing upright, I am learning how to run.

When I mention it to people, the most common reactions I get are "Why?" and "Isn't that bad for your joints?" But my favorite came from my ex-husband, who stared at me for a moment, laughed under his breath as he shifted his weight from one foot to the other and said "Huh, running . . . don't you already know how to do that?" Indeed.

I haven't any real desire to try my hand at ballet again, but there's still time for a writing career and an education and I sure would love to learn how to stop running from the difficulties inherent in any relationship. Maybe I can break through all of that "woulda, coulda, shoulda" by learning to push myself past this self-imposed mental and physical limit. I'm ready to let that weasel know it's time for her to dig a hole in someone else's field.

So I joined a gym four months ago and started with speed walking on the treadmill. I can do about an hour at anywhere from 4.2 to 4.7 mph. I'm six feet tall and in this instance it's pretty cool having long legs. It took a few times to get over the floating feeling that leaving the machine gives me—my first time I fell down a flight of steps because it felt like I was on an escalator. My confused brain did not know what to do with stationary stairs that my eyes and feet perceived as rushing towards me.

Now I'm comfortable on the treadmill and love the funky rhythm and stride I find, listening to Fatboy Slim on my headphones, butt tight and arms swinging. My endurance has increased considerably and one day a few weeks ago I wanted to push myself so I turned up the speed to 5.2 mph. I had to run, or suffer the humiliation of falling down and being shot across the room. I've seen it happen and it isn't pretty. I told myself to just do it for two minutes, then go back to walking. I did it. Two minutes, huffing like Puff the Magic Dragon on his deathbed, smoke pouring out of my ears. I had tunnel vision and my arms and legs went numb. I thought I might throw up. I was fairly certain that everyone in the gym had their eyes secretly trained on this spastic giraffe, expecting to see me make high-speed-full-contact with the mirror behind me.

I slowed my pace back to walking for a little longer and regained control of my breathing. Signaling the staff that I was fine and they could put the oxygen tank away, I got down and stretched. Oh dear Lord, my shins hurt. So did my calves, and my ankles, and my hips, and my thighs. Perhaps my shoes were a tad worn out, besides—they were cross-trainers, not runners.

Ah, the excuse the weasel was patiently waiting for—knowing full well it would come. This turn of events set me back a few weeks. Money's tight and running shoes aren't cheap. But in an effort to not let her win again, I began telling everyone and anyone who would listen that I am officially learning how to run.

I also checked out running sites online, where I got great tips on how to begin. The consensus was: walk fast, then run for two minutes. Of course, they recommend doing it in five-minute walk/two-minute run intervals for up to an hour. Then they suggest increasing each running interval by one minute every week until finally you are just running for the whole session. I was well on my way—once I got those running shoes, of course.

Exercising his great listening skills, my mate gave me cash for my birthday. He apologized for such an impersonal gift and promised that it wasn't that he didn't know what to get. He just has much larger feet, and can't possibly try shoes on for me.

I took that money to the mall with advice from the Internet swirling around in my head. "Buy from a store that employs athletes who have a strong knowledge of the products." I figured that would be a given at

Lady Foot Locker. Not so. The sixteen year-old staffers had overdeveloped thumbs and bodies shaped like couches. Definitely not runners. The salesgirl met all of my specific questions about fit and function with, "Um, I don't know." When I asked if anyone in that store might know how to properly fit a person with running shoes, she didn't know that either but was happy to tell me which ones were the most popular.

Grabbing my bag I trudged downstairs to the Discount Shoe Warehouse, where the aisles are long, and the selection is overwhelmingly large. There is no sales help, but no one bothers you either. I tried on about thirty pairs of shoes, and ran up and down the aisles in each one. Another customer, a big-haired woman in the metallic, strappy shoe aisle, looked at me walleyed every time I ran past. I relished seeing her hair stir in the breeze I created and I whispered "eat my dust" as I blew by. I felt like Flo-Jo but I'm sure I looked a whole lot more like The Road Runner, only slower, much slower.

I found my dream shoes, a pair of blue Asics that fit all of the strange curves of my feet where the other brands left gaps and made me worry about fallen arches and oozing blisters. I ran around the store a few more times just to be certain, and yes, they felt like an extension of my feet, just like the websites said they should. They felt nothing like the ballet toe shoes. I was one step closer to really learning how to run—brazenly ignoring the sniffling voice in my head.

I introduced my new running shoes to the gym and the treadmill for the first time yesterday morning. I really didn't want to go, I'm premenstrual, so my ligaments all felt loose and my muscles felt tired. I worried about injuring myself. But I've got these new shoes, and this expensive membership, and a desire to break this awful habit of starting something and then not finishing it just because it challenges me and makes me want to run away.

So I ran. I did two sets of two minutes each in a forty minute walk. My socks rubbed unmercifully against the tender flesh of my feet cradled in my comfy new shoes. That wasn't supposed to happen. I'll need to get some of those high-performance sport-fiber socks with techno-miracle wicking action. Was that my little weasel I heard, chewing on pieces of my motivation and self-confidence down there in her lair? I hissed at her to shut up and leave me alone, that I'm going to do this, blisters or no blisters.

I didn't much want to go to the gym today, either. But I did and I ran my two sets of two minutes, which is about all I can handle right now, especially until I settle this sock problem. Next week I will add in one more set, two if I feel adventurous. I felt I really deserved those ten minutes in the steam room after my workout, and I am hurting all over.

I see that roll of tummy hanging over the top edge of my jeans like a swollen lower lip, and I can't help but laugh. The weasel seems to be napping for the moment and I am writing and feeling safe in my body, even with all of these new aches and pains. I can hardly remember what I was so afraid of in the first place.

Just Keep Moving

Joanne Moniz

TIVERTON, RHODE ISLAND

February. The wind is stiff, brittle, and relentless. Depending upon your perspective, slate gray New England sky and naked tree branches are either bleak or poetic. The sun may not burn through until May. But I sit on my living room couch pulling on a purple sweatsuit, sneakers, and a knitted, rainbow-striped hat. I slide my two hundred-plus pound body onto the floor and lean over, hoping I'll touch my shins. My hips groan as they rotate, and my hamstrings slowly awaken from their eight-year hibernation. I hadn't asked them to do anything since basic training, and they were both surprised, and annoyed with my sudden demands.

I reach down my legs as far as my stomach's rolls will allow. I sit up and go down again. I bring my legs together and reach down again, this time sliding my hands just below my knees. I feel tension in my lower back and as I lean closer, squashing my abdomen, my sweatshirt crawls up my back. I drop my hands into my lap, slumped over, and look up through my basement apartment window. Here goes.

My first steps onto the road are tentative. I line up with the rock, my start and finish point, and check my Ironman watch. The chronograph reads all zeroes. I switch my Walkman on, touch the stopwatch button, and begin a slow shuffle over the cratered surface of Fairway Drive. My scarf covers mouth and nose as I set my arms in their half-bent position and bounce them loosely, forward and back, to meet the weak rhythm of my feet. The music blares in my ears and I focus on the voices to keep my mind off the torture I'm prepared to face as I embark on this quest to heal my damaged body and spirit.

Although I had spent my teen years in good shape, playing volleyball and tennis, and riding bikes, I didn't carry my youthful energy into adulthood. I had kept enough of it by the time I hit nineteen years old that I was able to pass my Army physical fitness tests in boot camp, but those scores steadily dropped during my enlistment in the National Guard. I hadn't the interest or discipline to force my body into performing the magic it had displayed in my youth.

I stagger along my running route, pre-designated and measured. I raise my arms and slide the cuff of my sweatshirt up; my arms meet the fogging lenses of my glasses. I'm nearly at the half-mile mark and my watch shows more than four minutes have elapsed. The seconds spin by, digital numbers changing too fast to read. I drop my arms and double-check my footing in the breakdown lane. I calculate my possible finish time. Six-minute half-miles. Twelve-minute miles. Twenty-four minutes for two miles. My best time in the army was 15:10. I taunt myself, and immediately feel disappointment weigh me down further, slowing my steps. But I beg myself, *just keep moving*.

I round the curve at my first half-mile and wish I had never left the house. Tears well up and spill out of the corners of my eyes. If I hadn't overeaten myself into this grotesque body I wouldn't be out in sub-zero weather setting myself up for another failure. *How am I going to do this?*

I try to focus on the music surrounding me. The singers take turns screaming at me through the headphones and I'm glad I brought them along, believing that, without them, the aloneness of running would kill me. I look around the neighborhood. Peering into the houses, I wonder how many people are behind the glass watching my head bob. Cars whiz by and I worry that the drivers are laughing at this huge woman plodding along in the breakdown lane of Stafford Road, scraping her shoe bottoms on the dirt pushed aside by hundreds of rolling tires. They're probably thinking something rude. Hey, *Dunkin Doughnuts is the other way! Why bother? You're gonna die anyway!* I'm grateful that my hat and scarf mask my features. They can't see who I am.

The first mile is nearly finished. I trudge up the hill, almost walking, and round the turn that hugs Arruda's Dairy Farm. The fresh manure smell slices through the frigid air and my nose runs faster. I rub the rough scarf against my face, mopping up the mess.

Arruda's silo sits far back from the road, and in the afternoon gray you can barely distinguish it from the sky behind it. I reach the tree that marks my mile. I dare not cheat myself, so I stumble a couple of yards beyond it and turn to head back home.

As I pivot around I remember my promise: Run the first mile, and I'll walk the second. But I don't really feel like walking. Sure, it'd be nice to be able to breath again, but I made the first mile. I made the first mile. I feel lighter. My feet practically lift themselves as I bounce downhill and past the silo again. I lose track of the music as I'm swept up in this accomplishment.

I fly past houses; they blur. Do the dwellers see me? I peer through fogged glasses at the cars rolling by. I recognize a white sedan and wave. It's Roberta from the store, and as she passes I see her crane her neck to look back at me. I hope she recognizes me. I smile beneath my knitted mask as my nose continues to drain. I drag the scarf across my face and resume my arm swing.

Each step propels me closer to home. I can feel my whole body moving now, not just my thick legs. The motion of my excess weight jumping around my bones unnerves me at first, but I begin to relax. At least it's moving. I gain more ground until I spy the house through the woods. Before I know it, an inner voice dares me to explode. I don't argue, as I dig the ball of my left foot into the pavement and launch my body into an all-out sprint. I pump each arm, forward and back, fists balled up, elbows tight into my sides. I gasp for oxygen but refuse to let up. The rock. The rock awaits me and I kick faster to meet it. I pass the rock, stop the clock, and stumble to a halt. I want to scream. I feel nauseous. My head swims as I suck in great gulps of air. I steady myself on my knees, bent over, red and sweating. *Keep moving—don't cramp up.* The steam puffing out of my nose and mouth makes me feel like a draft horse. I walk up the driveway.

In the house I peel layers of wet clothing away from my body. The sweatshirt reveals little about my exertion, but my t-shirt clings to my soaked back. The inside of my hat is wet, and I wring perspiration from my cloth watchband. I limp into the bathroom and stare at myself in the mirror. My face is so red my freckles look purple. My nostrils flare like an angry bull's. I stopped running five minutes ago and I still draw labored breath. My hair is drenched, and the sweat runs in rivers down my temples and neck. I leave the bathroom and stagger to the bedroom mirror—the full-length truth serum hanging on the door.

I'm still fat. I move closer to the glass and my vision narrows until all I see are two round, flaming cheeks and a couple of dark brown eyes. She's in there, I think. She will use this body, the one that trapped her, to set herself free.

Running Lessons

Kim Krolak

LATHAM, NEW YORK

I am not an athletic person by any stretch of the imagination. But I can honestly say that at this point in my life, running is good for my soul. Now, I say that as a mature, thirty-one-year-old single mom who has survived many hardships in her life, including the death of a child. I'm officially a grown-up and I can say things like "good for the soul." It hasn't always been that way.

Even though running has seemed to be pretty much a constant throughout my life, I haven't always had this "I run to seek inner peace" attitude. I don't always have it now. The following stories chronicle the life-changing experiences I have had as they relate to running. Each story represents a life lesson I was being taught at the time, and they chronicle my progress in running and life.

Lesson # 1: Be willing to fail (but do it with dignity).

It was Field Day. Sixth grade. I placed last in the fifty-yard dash to the sound of cruel laughter from my peers. I knew I was slow, but *someone* has to be last, right? Was it really that hysterical? My only trusted friend that year discreetly took me aside after the hellish event was over, and revealed the source of the ridicule: my feet kicked out to the sides behind me as I ran. Picture a twelve-year-old female Jerry Lewis impersonator gaily running the fifty-yard dash. Funny, huh. But I was mortified. I so wanted to be cool. I panicked. Is this fixable? Would I have to forcibly vomit every day we were to run in Phys. Ed.? I could not let on to these kids that I was indeed not cool. That was totally unacceptable. Well, this was going to change. The next time I lost a race, by God my legs would be straight.

Lesson #2: Never let 'em see you sweat, cry, look stupid, find out you're not perfect, or do anything else to let on you're a human being.

In high school Gym class we were introduced to the track. The big leagues. The almighty high school track. Over time, God had listened to my desperate prayers and my legs straightened out. I actually enjoyed running. I never did join the track team or become remotely fanatic about it—I just liked it. You didn't have to socialize or even speak to anybody, and I definitely preferred it to any team sport. You see, I never really was a "team player."

I took this interest outside of school. My mom and one of our neighbors (both housewives) decided to join the jogging craze of the 80s and run during the evenings. This way it was too dark for other neighbors to get a good look at what was jiggling as they ran. Those are my mom's words—not mine. In any event, it sounded good to me. I was not overweight, but extremely self-conscious nonetheless. Must have something to do with the Jerry Lewis incident.

Lesson #3: Always wear makeup—you never know who you'll run into.

Those evening runs proved to be a social endeavor as much as a physical one. I remember the night I ran into (okay, he ran into me) the boy across the street. He was about five years older than I was and was out walking. (I think he knew I was out and wanted some advice.) He was contemplating his recent marriage proposal to his girlfriend (they're now divorced). I have no recollection of what I told him, but we enjoyed each other's company anyway.

Lesson #4: If you can't be with the one you love, meet him in the woods.

Yes, this is quite possibly my favorite of my pre-enlightenment lessons. When I was fifteen, I ran at night with the hopes that my star-football-player-boyfriend might throw me a crumb and notice how tight my body was looking in my Bon Jours. Of course, I had to call him before I went running to make my whereabouts known to him. He just loved me so much, he had to know what I was doing at all times, you see. He would call after a reasonable time had passed to make sure I returned and was tucked safely in my parents' home for the night. Sweet, isn't it? . . . Or perhaps he caught on to the fact that I was running down the street to meet up with the boy that I *really* loved so we could make out in a patch of woods that someone has since dared to build a house upon? Who's to say? You know, I always did hate football.

Lesson #5: Take baby steps.

I stopped running when I was a teenager. I explored aerobics, weight training, step aerobics, yoga—you name it since then. I have also since experienced marriage, abuse, grief, divorce, parenthood, love, betrayal and more. It was only after my boy from the woods recently told me he went on his run past my parents' house one night that I remembered, "Hey, *I* used to enjoy running." No, we were not meeting in the woods again sixteen years later (damn), just communicating via e-mail. Anyway, the first time I got myself out of the house (not an easy task), it was like I always knew it to be. But I have to get myself out the door. How do I convince myself I wouldn't rather veg on the couch a little longer? I don't. I'm honest with myself. Sort of. I just tell myself I'm just going out for a leisurely walk. No pressure, no goal. Baby steps. Get the sneakers on and walk out the door. Once I'm out, I allow myself to run to the end of the street and resume walking again. This seems to work, for nine times out of ten, I end up running anyway.

Lesson #6: If you don't leave your house today, you may miss something wonderful.

The problem with working in your home, or getting involved in a book or movie like I do, is that you forget. I dragged myself out the door recently on a beautiful, crisp fall day. The sun was shining, it was about sicty-five degrees, and my son was at preschool. However, after a week of job interviews and no job in sight, I was a little tense. And when I get tense, I veg. I veg because anything else is too overwhelming. After a much needed suggestion from a friend, I chose to immerse myself in the sights, sounds and smells of my neighborhood. I felt particularly aware that day of the smell of a freshly sealed driveway, the aroma of wet leaves, and the vibrant colors of autumn. I was having a Peace Walk. I was calm immediately. As I did my walk/run, I passed an elderly gentleman who was taking out his trash. He paused as he saw me, wished me good morning, and commented on what a beautiful day it was. I agreed—yes, it is. I carried that smile he gave me for another block. And I still had it as I stopped around the corner to catch a dainty yellow butterfly landing upon a dandelion. Simple. A simple greeting from a man I don't even know. A simple yet beautiful act of nature. Two experiences I never would have had if I had chosen to see who the guests were on Montel Williams that morning.

Lesson #7: Running is good anger management.

I thank my ex-husband for frequently reminding me why I left him. And I thank him for keeping me in shape. During a counseling session a year ago, my counselor asked me where my anger goes. I had no clue what she was talking about. Don't get me wrong—I knew I was angry. I had good reason to be. However, I never considered the fact that anger needs an outlet. For if that anger doesn't come out somewhere, it eventually festers inside—thus my depression. By taking control of my own life and not trying to control his, I found a great power. When he ticked me off, I could take care of myself by getting out and going for a run—therapy on all levels.

Lesson #8: If it helps, do it.

This is very simply where I am now. From time to time I pamper myself (not often enough) and soak in a bubble bath by candlelight, or listen to music while enjoying the scent of lilac incense—anything that makes me feel good. I now consider running to be a luxury, for it is something I treat myself to. I sleep better, I'm getting fresh air, I'm relieving stress, and as a bonus my body gets firmer. I'm not trying to impress someone with my figure, and there's no mystery man I'm meeting around the block (damn again).

I run for me. Because it's good for my soul. Because it changed my life.

Tomorrow Might Not
Be the Same

Mina Foster

NEW YORK, NEW YORK

When I was twenty-seven I started running. I had run before; short struggles with the sidewalk and the occasional hills punctuated by moments of near asphyxiation as I gasped desperately to fill my lungs with oxygen. I was fit, at least as much as anyone else is. I had done aerobics for years after all. I was used to the outdoors in a city-girl way. I had been a camp counselor, although that was a decade earlier, and since then I had retreated into school, then work, suits, and late-night dinners at the office. But a series of three unrelated health crises, not mine, drove me out onto the roads for good.

It all started when my best friend Jamie dropped out of the sky onto a startled farmer in an Ontario vineyard (of chardonnay grapes), shattering her right heel beyond repair in a half-day parasailing lesson gone badly wrong. Her foot became a weather beacon, able to predict rain and damp with startling accuracy and painful swelling.

A few months later another friend, Olivia, gave birth to her first child, a daughter. The girl was healthy and happy, in the ninety-fifth percentile of every infant testing category important to her parents. Olivia did not top the charts in her recovery though. A crippling version of post-natal diabetes rendered her wheelchair-bound within the year. She grew frail, a shadow version of her former self. Not long afterwards my upstairs neighbor, Kathleen, was stricken with an insidious rheumatoid arthritis, stiffening and puffing up her joints, immobilizing her on days she indulged in anything with a whiff of dairy. She who once reveled in the sensual pleasures of cheddar and brie and ice cream.

Jamie, Olivia, Kathleen. They were all young, healthy and vibrant. Their lives revolved around budding careers in law, architecture and medicine. The future was theirs, but it was just that—in the future. When they had time, they were going to do the things they really enjoyed, get more exercise, go on long trips, paint. For now they were building their lives. They were working on the foundation. It took time. But they were young and time was infinite. Life wasn't much fun yet, but it would be.

And then it wouldn't be. The tomorrow-rug was pulled right out from underneath them. Suddenly there were only the would'ves and the gonnas. Theirs became lives lived as would-have-beens. I would've run a marathon. I was gonna go whitewater canoeing in the Northwest Territories. I would've climbed El Capitan. I was gonna learn to snowboard. Would've, gonna, would've, gonna. The chant repeated itself, evidentiary concerns aside. There was no evidence, no past history, to suggest that they were actually planning to take up running, or white water canoeing, or anything else for that matter. But when the opportunity was no longer available, how much sweeter it looked, how much more attainable, how much more desirable. Their regret for things that might have been was sharper than it was for what had actually been.

I took stock of me. I was an unhappy lawyer who worked too many hours. I was a moderately healthy gym rat. Like my friends, the list of adventures and achievements I only dreamed of was as long as my arm and as unlikely to be accomplished as walking on the sun: run a marathon, climb a mountain, go backpacking, travel to Africa, write a novel.

I needed a change. I didn't want to join the chorus of the would've, gonna choir. I needed a catalyst, a spark to ignite the tinderbox of fear filled by friends laid low, time run short.

I had recently moved to New York from Toronto and was proud that I had started running a little. I had worked up the courage and the endurance to run a whole loop of Central Park, almost ten kilometers in one shot. I was still adjusting to living with the old imperial measurement system of miles and ounces and quarts.

A woman I knew vaguely and was trying to befriend asked me about my running. Oh I run about ten, three times a week, I said airily. I was somewhat intimidated by her. She had run marathons. Inconceivable. I had in fact only run three times in a week once, but had determined that I should do it more often, so I felt only mildly guilty at telling her it was already an established habit. Wow, she said, you're really serious about running, that's great. I walked away feeling the pleasant pricklings of pride until I realized she thought 'ten' meant ten miles, not ten kilometers. I had never run ten miles in my life. Could I? Could I even run ten miles? I'd told a bald faced lie it seemed, unwittingly, but I was embarrassed.

I went home. Put on my shorts and shoes and went to the park. I did one loop, ten kilometers, or six miles as I was now trying to think of it. I did a second loop.

My feet hurt. My hips felt misaligned. Salt caked my temples. My skin tingled. My hair stood on end. My lungs opened up and I breathed in an entire world at my disposal.

I was addicted. It could have been the endorphins, but I think it was and is more. It's the pure pleasure. It's rain, snow or shine. It's dark mornings and sunny afternoons. It's exploring a new city or a forest path. It's freedom and strength. It's joy.

I had always wanted to do a marathon, but had barely admitted it even to myself. Now, I thought as I finished my first twelve-mile run, I will.

I did.

And I went to Africa and backpacked to the top of Kilimanjaro. I wrote a novel, maybe I'll write two.

And I run. It's not a would've or a gonna. I do. And I do. And I do. Because I love it and because I'm scared that tomorrow might not be the same as today and if something happens to me I'll still have what I did, not just what I was going to do. I don't want to be late for my dreams. I want to live now, not buried under the heavy earth-weight of worries and responsibilities, waiting for spring, waiting for my life to begin.

Mo(u)rning Run

Courtney E. Cole

BINGHAMTON, NEW YORK

In Memory of P. Christian Cole (1945-1999)

The news came slower than it seemed it should have. I felt, afterward, that any message so tragic should have come in a revelatory instant. But the words dribbled in a slow whisper off my brother's tongue and hung suspended across the phone line between us. "He's gone."

Gone. I spent the next few months trying to absorb the reality of my father's sudden death in a motorcycle accident. Gone. Dead. The words echoed incessantly in my mind, which could focus on little else. The rest of the semester remains a blur of trauma and shock. I do remember driving from college in St. Louis to Santa Fe. The Texas panhandle was less awful than I'd imagined. Actually, it was quite enchanting, with its highway medians covered in tangles of windblown wildflowers. I arrived two days later in Santa Fe to spend the summer together with my father's wife. That was the summer I started running.

It was clear that I was emotionally unprepared for his death. Barely twenty-one, I was distraught at the inexplicable loss of my father. One June afternoon, it was just too much. I was overwrought and tired of crying. There was so much pain and anger that the tears never released and these feelings planted themselves in uncomfortable knots that settled in the back of my throat, itching to be freed. I was beside myself. Not knowing what else to do, I threw on a sports bra and laced up my sneakers. It was an impulsive decision, without much forethought. But one afternoon followed that first day in June, and another and another, until the days connected together into a skeleton of successive runs.

It worked. I finally had an outlet. All the negative sensations I was experiencing finally had some place to go, at least for those forty-five minutes a day. Not just a release from them, but their redemption. I learned that when I ran, I could wear my grief in public. In offering my mourning to the intense heat of the New Mexican summer afternoon, my tears were indistinguishable from sweat.

The framework of my emotional convalescence can be traced in the pattern of running shoe footprints. I'd come home from work and change into my shorts and T-shirt and move out into the streets and dirt roads of the city. I didn't focus on running fast or keeping track of the distances covered. I just ran—I moved my left foot forward, then my right foot, again and again in a fraternal, almost jovial two-count beat. My arms moved opposite my legs in a similar, if silent, pace. The rhythm of my breathing created a counterpoint, another cadence of my running. There was simplicity in the regulated movements, the tempo of arms, legs, and breath working together to make my body move forward, a pace at a time. The motion of running created a disciplinary conduit in which the pain, anger, disbelief, grief, sadness, frustration, vacuity, and bitterness melted and transformed. It was an endeavor of active mourning, by which all of the anguish was converted into physical movement that left me, at run's end, feeling exhausted and purified.

The pain of my father's death has softened and the moments of overwhelming grief come less often now, though still unpredictably. I run everyday, and this daily ritual remains forever intertwined with the abrupt death of my father. I have better and worse days with each. Sometimes my body feels lithe and vibrant with the memory of this man, the beauty of his existence merging with my own as I move. Other days,

I have to fight for every step, a painful reminder of mortality, and my tears—like so many runs before—blend with my body's sweat. But no matter what, that time I spend running leaves me feeling uplifted by the spirit of my father and closer to his memory, cherishing the promise of another day. Each morning, when I settle into the rhythm of my running shoes, their alternating touch on the pavement, I am reminded—both physically and emotionally—of the transformative force of running in my life since Dad's death.

Above all I retain an abiding sense of the redemptive power of running. It is an activity that takes my pain and confusion and burns them, like some alternative fuel, into energy for movement. People always want to know, "How do you do it?" They think that running everyday is a result of willpower, an ability to stick to a disciplinary regime. My willpower is irrelevant and my answer simple. I run because I always feel better at the end. That is the uncomplicated reason for my daily running regimen. Running maintains its transformative role in my life, still, years after my father's death. Its role continues to be one of resolution—of emotional quagmires, mental unrest, spiritual doubts—rather than a physical preoccupation with distance or speed.

Running remains an activity of morning—where my being, in time with footsteps, connects intensely with my memory of Dad and the pain of the emptiness his death occasioned. Through pace and pore, in the contemplative, measured steps of my morning run, I have learned to escape the corporeal confines of the painful loss of my parent. But I have also found freedom, and not just escape. Running has allowed me to indulge in heartache fully, and to move, in steps, beyond it. When the winter air of upstate New York burns its chill into my lungs and my limbs tingle pink in the morning's cold embrace and I struggle happily through another morning run, I am reminded that I have felt pain in its rawest and most intense forms and I have also found a way beyond this pain. My steps echo across the empty morning, a testament of defiant redemption, and I know that running has changed me forever. In the months and miles since my father's death, despite such irreparable loss, I have been freed to experience joyfulness again.

Hustle

Matt Dinniman

TUCSON, ARIZONA

My first track meet.

I was fourteen. Yes, it was only junior varsity. I was a freshman after all, and as far as I was concerned, I was damn lucky just to be on the team. The sun was unnaturally hot for so early in the year. Every salty, burning stream of sweat off my forehead seemed to zero in on the inside corner of my eye, stinging. It was the first time I had actually worn the school track uniform, and the tank-top felt strange on my skinny shoulders, like it would slip off either side and my shirt would drop down, past my shorts, to my ankles. I was constantly fidgeting, grabbing at my shoulder straps. The spikes on my feet were odd too. They bit into the ground more than they did at my school's track. Like in those dreams where you had to flee, but you were hopelessly mired in molasses.

It wasn't a question if I was going to lose or not. I already knew I was to come in last place. Everyone on my team knew. It was how badly I was going to lose that worried me.

Two-hundred meters isn't that far. Not really. It's only half the track. In practice, it wasn't so bad, though I suspect some of my friends would deliberately slow down, just so I could say it was close. I barely noticed them when I ran. The coach, a huge man with a handlebar mustache and a slight smell of locker room permanently mixed in with his breath, would scream that word at them, at me.

Hustle! Hustle!

I barely noticed that, too.

But at track practice, there weren't two hundred spectators. The crisp new uniforms that slipped off your shoulders. The strange faces of the other teams. The early morning smell. The constant report of the starting gun.

My father sitting in the stands.

God, I was scared. As my race neared, I began to question what I was doing here. Why I submitted myself to the daily, after-school disgrace that was track practice. Why I was about to submit myself to the even worse humiliation of shaming myself in front of both strangers and my father.

"Why do you do it?" my friend Tim had asked one day after the first week of practice. I had been home twenty minutes, and I was still broken on my bed, tongue lolling out like a dog.

"I like it," I answered. "It's fun."

He grunted. "Doesn't look fun to me."

The gun cracked. I ran.

I imagined the invisible staircase as I rose from the blocks, just as I had been taught. I felt light as air. My legs were pistons. I pushed against my very limits, until I felt something inside of me rip and tear away, and I was going faster than I had ever gone before. I ran. I ran.

I ran.

Afterwards, my father came down from the stands. I was still bent over hands on knees. He put his heavy hand on my shoulder.

"You did great."

I looked up, surprised. He was a big man, strong and muscled. Good at everything.

"I came in last place."

"What does that have to do with anything?"

Coach walked up, shook hands with my father. "He's not the fastest on the team, but everyone feeds off his passion."

My father nodded, as if Coach had been stating the obvious.

Coach went on. "We have high hopes for him."

Father slapped me on the back again. "If he threw the energy he gives to his running into his school work, we'd have a valedictorian on our hands."

They laughed and spoke some more. I looked between them, mouth agape. They *had* to be talking about someone else. Either that, or they'd both gone mad.

Later that night, I looked "passion" up in the dictionary. *Something that is desired intensely*. I thought about that. I enjoyed running. I wasn't too fond of losing every single race, but it was the price I had to pay in order to do what I loved. Sure, I could do it alone, but I needed the coach and his advice, the camaraderie of my fellow runners. Most of them didn't care how fast or how slow I was.

I learned something important that day. You can't choose your passions. No matter how hard you try. They choose you. I feel so lucky that mine is something as simple as running. Sure, I'm much better at plenty of other things. But doing well at something you're naturally good at isn't that big of a feat. Trying your best, even when you know you're going to fail, that's where the true challenge lies. I think about that every day.

As the years of high school passed, I stayed in track, determined. I suffered several last-place finishes. I moved from sprints to distance to hurdles and back to sprints again. I enjoyed them all. The sprints were like bite-sized explosions of everything you had. For me, it wasn't speed so much as being able to take every ounce of energy in your entire soul and transfer it to that moment. So much so that you collapse at the very end. The distance races were much different, but I loved them all the same. Taking that energy and spreading it out just right. I joined the cross country team as well, and during the summers I hit the desert trails almost every day as the sun was rising. I competed in five and ten Ks. As my body adjusted to the constant conditioning, I improved greatly. Though I never did win a race. Not even once.

I run almost every day. Not because I have to. Not because I want to stay in great shape—though that doesn't hurt. I enjoy it. It makes me happy. It is my passion. *My* passion. But it's more than that too. I race in order to keep my humility, to remind me that you must take the good with the bad, you have to hustle sometimes, even if it means coming in last, despite your greatest efforts. Otherwise you won't ever truly be happy.

Compulsory Exercise

Dean Liscum

SUGAR LAND, TEXAS

I run because I have to, because I can't not run. Running smoothes the rough edges of my mind. It calms my nerves. Its *gros movement* dissipates the energy that builds up in my hips and shoulders. Each step loosens the tension on the sinews in my calves and quadriceps. On a day I don't run, I am irritable and petulant. I worry about small, insignificant details that pile up in the corners of my life. I rearrange things: furniture in the living room, toys in my sons' rooms, stacks of papers on my desk, tools in the garage. My fingers worry over everything they touch as if objects were prayer beads in a nun's hands. I run my finger over and over a slight ridge on my wife's scalp or pick at ridge on her nail. I feel compelled to move things around, shake things up. These are mindless acts of mixing and reordering, but I do them in spite of knowing this. As I sit, my hamstrings twitch and my buttocks ache. My feet tap out the rhythm of the song on the radio or the cadences of Silvia Poggioli's voice on N.P.R. or the whirring of the dishwasher.

Running was always a part of my life, implicit, omnipresent. Others recognized this fact and made it manifest. As a child I was always running inside the house and running into things: coffee tables, siblings, open refrigerator doors, dollhouses, bar stools, adults with cocktails, Lego towers. So, I was sent outside to run more and to run into bigger and less fragile things. At the urging of a baseball coach, my father took me to a local high-school track where a Junior Olympics track club worked out. I was eleven.

I run because of two facts of the physical act of running: you fly and it hurts.

To say that to run is to fly sounds sensational, but it's true. Running is an act in which you are intentionally, perpetually, gracefully propelling yourself towards the heavens and then falling earthward. You thrust your body upward and forward beyond a point of vertical equilibrium with one leg, your momentum carries you forward, and gravity pulls you toward the pavement. You extend your other leg out to break your fall. Your ankle pivots, your hip rotates, your calf and knee flex and extend to transfer your weight in the direction of the momentum, at which point you leap upward and forward again.

It is this brief instance of being airborne, of the suspension of the body over the ground that rotates ever so slightly beneath you, this detachment, this momentary sensation of floating freely repeated hundreds of times a minute that constitutes flight. On a smaller scale, proportional to my arc through the air, this flight gives me the same rising, dislocating sensation that I feel on a roller coaster as it begins to descend the highest slope and I begin to leave my seat.

This elation is measured in fragments of a second. The feeling, repeating in rapid succession, pressing against the mind in contiguous slivers of time, flickers across the consciousness like an old movie. The mind edits out the fleeting moments on the ground like the sidebars of each frame in the film. It forgets or ignores mundane details of running: foot strike, leg height, arm position. It quits monitoring breathing, heartbeat, blood flow. You glide past suburban landscape of mailboxes, parked cars, basketball goals, past the day-to-day detritus of family, work, and life. You experience only the flight.

Some days it doesn't work. Some days are pure drudgery. A thousand steps. A thousand false starts. A thousand failed attempts to fly. A thousand times of falling back to earth. You do it, not necessarily because you're certain or even confident that you will fly again, but because you have flown, because your mind understands the risks and knows the possibilities of both success and failure, and because some days the hope that you will fly is enough.

The physics of running, like the physics of flight, make running a dangerous act. The runner is constantly in a precarious state of being balanced and yet off balance. It is little more than a controlled fall: a leaping and catching yourself and leaping again. It is throwing yourself off balance for the pure, dizzying pleasure. It is a pure form of flux, of controlled change. With this constant disorienting and reorienting, this controlled destabilization, comes pain and injury.

If you run far enough, fast enough, hard enough, eventually this activity gets to you. You destroy something. Runners are always in pain or injured. Shin splints, side cramps, bone spurs, blackened toenails, strained tendons, strained arches. It's the ticket price of low-orbit flying.

Running hard and fast is particularly painful. It hurts. I learned to do it in the Texas heat as a child on that Junior Olympics track team. We would run intervals—200s, 400s, and 800s—until we couldn't run any more.

"How many?" we'd ask the coach, a tall, laconic black man who'd run the 400-meter hurdles in college.

"Until I get tired of standing here," he'd say without smiling.

"How fast?"

"As fast as you can," the coach would say and then look off into the curve and work the toothpick in his mouth, "and then a little faster."

Our feet blistered. Our lungs burned. Our practice uniforms were soaked with sweat. Our shoes squished.

At the finish line, the sprint coach, a compact, muscular woman who looked like she was going to blast into the sky when she demonstrated how to use the starting block, would threaten the sprinters. "Run through the line and don't complain about the pain. If you want to feel pain, I'll make you run with the middle-distance runners."

The Texas high school I attended didn't know what to do with a middle-distance runner. Tall, skinny athletes were either wide receivers or basketball players. The coaches were football coaches first and whatever else second. At the start of the school year, they must have drawn straws for track. I wound up with an ex-collegiate lineman who probably weighed 400 pounds when his diet was working. He showed up on time and was enthusiastic. That was the extent of his coaching skills.

Usually, he'd ask me what I thought the workout should be, and because I liked to fly, I chose 800- or 400-meter intervals or 1000-meter stairs with 200-meter increments. He'd agree and mop his face with a white gym towel, intone "On your mark. Get set. Go!" and start the watch. I'd stumble to the finish line after each interval, and before I could catch my breath the coach was calling me up to the starting line. He had a wise-ass, carnival manner about him and was always pontificating about something or other for the entertainment of the girls' track team or the cheerleaders practicing on the football field inside the track.

He'd always beckon me to the starting line with "Step up to the line and . . . " finishing with some inane phrase like "pay the lady," "kiss the cow," "show the women what you're made of," or "face the music." Generally, I blocked it out, along with girls' track team members adjusting their shorts as they stretched for what seemed like hours, and the cheerleaders tumbling across the infield until they were too dizzy to stand, and the sprinters complaining that they didn't need to run all that much, just lift weights and do the leg speed drills. Once, however, when I had just started running 400-meter intervals and wasn't yet into it, I was half listening to him mouth off. He said, "Step up to the line and talk to god." I looked into his sweating, smiling face for some sort of clarification, because neither of us was particularly religious. I thought maybe he was teasing me, because I was teenage-strident about the fact I was a non-practicing Catholic. I knew all coaches got religious before games and when someone got seriously hurt, but neither condition applied in this instance. His expression didn't change as he started me off.

"Go."

I did. Assuming there is a god and it made us, and by using what we've been given we honor or praise that god, then I talked to god—pumping my arms, driving my legs, regulating my breath, trying to keep an even pace, fighting to keep my arms from going slack, forcing my legs from slowing down as the muscles screamed for mercy. It was a simple prayer spoken in motion. My sinews were the words; my bones, the sentences. The synapses spoke the syllables, the cartilage supplied the chorus. That day, running became conversation with the infinite.

Running changed my life in that it gave it shape and made it possible. Running is one of the few activities in which you push yourself to your physical limit, where pure exertion cannot be replaced by skill or finesse, where you can't fake it (and if you do it right, you wouldn't want to), where you find yourself saying, "I can't go on," and in the next step saying, "I'll go on." And you do.

Runner

Sharon Reidy

SAN DIEGO, CALIFORNIA

"Right, left, keep going" ... *"Watch out for those roots!"* ... *"Aargh, these roots are gonna kill me!"* ... *"Why in the world am I doing this, I can quit, I don't have to keep going."* ... *"When is this gonna end?"* ... *"My lungs are gonna explode if I don't stop soon!"* The thoughts roared in my ears, louder even than my heart's *"thuumpa, thuump, thuumpa."* Something inside me would not quit, I couldn't stop yet, I had to finish the run. *"Calm down, Laine, breathe deep. It's not that far, you're almost half-way ..."* Calming thoughts helped somewhat at first, but they increasingly lost ground to the pain filling my consciousness—from my shins, a wrenched knee, my throat and my lungs.

The trail twisted among the island's scrub pine. Even in July, dawn brought light but little warmth to northern Maine. In the chill air, my breath trailed as a jet stream in my wake. Doubt, fear, fatigue, and the overwhelming desire to quit filled my mind with confusion, but with every step the noise lessened until all fused into a single thought—keeping up with the body in front of me. I never even wondered who that body might be. It was simply a moving target. I matched it step for step, never letting the distance between us shrink or grow beyond two to three yards. I was its nemesis. It could not lose me.

That day stands out for me. You see, each day that run had been inflicted on me, and I hated it. Every morning I begged to be exempted. I didn't want to run and worried that the rocks and snags would twist my ankles or hurt my weak knees. Running seemed an unnecessary chore to me, something to be avoided. The Outward Bound Staff on Hurricane Island had different ideas, however, and gently but firmly directed me to move my caboose down the trail with the rest of the group. So I extracted a subtle revenge—I always hung back in last place, frequently slowing to a walk, and rarely exerting myself to any real effort.

For three weeks I fought my silent (and possibly unnoticed) war. Then something altogether unexpected happened. Perhaps I slept better (or worse) than usual or maybe something in the food bolstered me or a good spirit floated down from on high—I will never know the reason. That day I woke up and determined to change, and that run affected me so that now, twenty years later, I still see that morning as pivotal in my life.

Yet, it is difficult to say exactly what changed. It hurt to run those one and a half miles, far more than I believed possible. The cold air, the twisty turns and fast pace challenged my determination, coordination, strength and stamina to their limits. I gasped for breath like a fish out of water while my fair skin turned a greenish hue. Time and again, meanwhile, I pushed thoughts of quitting aside and refocused my mind on the body in front of me. As long as that body moved, so would I, right to the finish line.

As we neared the end, the body moved forward at an even faster pace. My strength nearly expended, I struggled to keep up, but the distance grew between us. Then, incredibly, instead of stopping at the finish line, it kept going. *"No!"* I shouted with all my remaining strength, *"I can't do it! I can't go any farther."* I cried out loud in my frustration and rage as I crossed the line. The body continued ahead unmoved. I still remember how it pained me to breathe. The muscles in my chest and abdomen cramped, my breath came in great gasps which no amount of oxygen seemed to calm. Sweat poured off my body which felt curiously cold and clammy. I felt faint and nauseous. Even the knowledge of having achieved my goal and a few compliments by friends did not make me feel much better.

Hours later, sitting by the fire warming myself with a good oatmeal breakfast and hot coffee after our cold morning swim, I was surprised by the approach of Kim, one of the instructors. A youngish woman, probably in her late twenties, she impressed me with her upbeat attitude, drive, and energy. She was a true runner. She liked marathons, speed, competition, challenge, all the hallmarks of a Type-A personality, yet with heart and common sense. She walked purposefully toward me. I noticed a funny look on her face but could not place the expression. As she spoke, I searched my conscience for misdeeds. She began by telling me that she had led our run that morning. I realized then that I had never identified the body in front of me. Her news impressed me, she was a good runner. Then I learned that she, too, had made a resolution that morning—she had decided to run her fastest time. Her expression changed to a mixture of doubt and wonder as she told me that the footsteps behind her had challenged her to put everything she had into the run. Later, she had wanted to learn the identity of these footsteps. Without wanting to insult me, she conveyed that she had never imagined I could be that person and had not at first believed it.

I'm glad she took the time to approach me that morning. She taught me something very important. There is something within me (and all of us) which is capable of doing great things—things unexpected and unbelievable. Having reflected much on this, I know the key was that one moment when I decided to let go of my bad attitude and reach out towards a healthy goal. To challenge myself rather than embed myself in pointless rebellion or fears of injury. That run changed my life because I experienced some very basic truths—pain is just pain, fear is just fear, and negativity pulls one down. The only thing holding me back was my own poor attitude; once this changed so did my potential to succeed. Many times I have thought back to the lessons learned that morning, and the memory has encouraged me to push through fear and negativity, to go after a difficult goal, and to go through pain for a good purpose. That, to me, is health. What better gift could one receive?

Just Play

Christy Thomas

TUCSON, ARIZONA

I was in the fifth grade and it was a sunny summer Sunday afternoon. My mom also taught the fifth grade at the time and one of her favorite students was Craig Blandford. My mom wasn't ashamed that she had favorites. I remember hearing about them during dinner. Craig Blandford was one of them. Craig happened to live on the next street behind Butler Place, my little cul-de-sac.

That Sunday afternoon, Craig stopped by. I was in the fifth grade and had only a hazy, tentative notion of boys up until that afternoon. Craig rang the doorbell. I answered. The clearest liquid blue eyes that I had ever seen—the blue of Caribbean seas—met my gaze. Smitten, I ran to get Mom. I did not know this boy but I knew mom did. Mom introduced us and then, almost immediately, as kids will do, we took off to play. The beautiful thing about play at that age is that there is no plan in mind, no place to get to, just the vague but decisive idea of play.

I think Craig made the play call. And I quickly found out that there was a whole world of boys just blocks away, having adventures right beyond my backyard. Capture the flag, king of the mountain, HORSE, and others were games I never knew existed before that summer. I transformed into a tomboy so I could be with Craig. Whatever Craig did, I wanted to do. That first afternoon, we met three of his friends and ran 2.1 miles, timed with a stopwatch. I had never considered running before. But if Craig was running, I was going to run. Practically every other day that summer, we ran the same two-mile road route that Craig and his buddies mapped out. One day, he announced that it was better to breathe through your nose than through your mouth. Therefore, we all needed to fill our mouths up with water and run the entire two miles without drinking or otherwise losing the water. At the end of the run, we would show our success by spitting it out. Okay, I said, because whatever Craig wanted to do seemed perfect to me. I still remember that run. It was brutal, especially on a ten-year-old.

Craig Blandford and I went on one date when we were sixteen years old and he was captain of his football team and I was co-captain of my track team. He was self-conscious that night, I remember, because he had split his chin open on the football field and required stitches. He was still drop-dead handsome to me. We have never felt as awkward as that night, when we tried to formally date. He brought me a rose, I blushed, and at the end of the evening, he bent over to give me a good night kiss. We reeled back from that kiss and blushed. We both felt the same. For me it was like kissing my brother.

Directly after college, some of my best friends and I went up to New York City and became bankers, investment bankers, and other incarnations of success, or what I viewed as success back then. We worked on Wall Street and we worked hard. My roommate in New York worked at Goldman Sachs as an investment banker. She was very athletic. She ran often. She hated it. She never understood how I could get so lost in thought during a run that I would often not know what mile marker I was on or how far I had to go. She always knew exactly where she was in her run. Apparently, this difference bothered her and she put a lot of thought into it. One night she came home after a run around the reservoir in Central Park and she said she had figured out the difference between us with running. She said, "Christy, I've always run to get in shape for something else. Field hockey, soccer, lacrosse." For her, running was a means to an end. For me, it was the end itself.

Running is my meditation, my relaxation. It is the time I designate to sort through things in my life and gain clarity. I compose letters during my runs, I rehash conversations I have with co-workers during my runs, I think about what I will say to my mom on the phone during those runs, I recently composed the speech I would give at my dad's retirement party on a run.

I am now thirty-six years old and have left New York. I have been co-captain of my high school track team, I have run races here in Tucson, I have placed in those races, and I am headed out the door to run eight miles in a few minutes. I have run almost every single day since that first day Craig Blandford knocked on my door.

Craig lives in Alaska now with his wife. I haven't talked to him in years. But my mom called me on my birthday recently and told me that I had received a very special phone message. Mom and Dad were out but Craig had called to wish me a happy birthday. Our birthdays are two days apart. I always think of him then but had no idea he still remembered. His spirit of play and love of running, from all those years ago, changed my life.

Running and Wings

Sally Blue Wakeman

NEW YORK, NEW YORK

Wings are everywhere today—in my feet, in my lungs, in the cloud, in the legs of the women runners around me. The cloud is huge like the span of an eagle's weight, and it covers the sun. The sweat on my legs rubs and stings me as I sit here cross-legged in Central Park, after having run its circumference. Resting, I watch a broken butterfly. It opens its wings to the light. I think: perhaps this is the last time it shall ever perform its sun worship, for surely it is near death. Musty gray incense dust falls in whorls from its brown, intricately designed wings. It stumbles blindly through the grass. Doesn't it know that it needs the nectar of flowers, not dry cut weeds, to survive? It shivers and quakes. Its blindness and befuddlement over its own mortality mirrors my own. Like me, it tries to find warmth by spreading wings and breathing hard; its veins, like mine, thrum wildly in its body after flight.

I look up and I see another young woman in the distance. She is lying on her back in the grass. She lifts a leg, high; her limbs are as slender and strong as reeds. She bends gently, and then releases; she lifts the other leg. I know what she feels like as she stretches; this woman may as well be me, repeated. She is engaging in a ritual before she runs, much the way the butterfly does.

There is another woman on the bench, watching me. Her stomach paunch sweats and heaves. She is uncomfortable within the immensity of her own weight. Perhaps running helps her to lighten herself, as it does for me. And there are others here, absorbing the heat of the sun and pulse of the earth. Breath lifts breasts; invisible wings open and close like lungs. Although this is the city, I believe I can smell a river drying. I wiggle my toes. In my body there is the sensation of gentle lifting. I am springing upward inside, as if the weight of snow has fallen from my bough.

We all sit privately in our solitudes. I exude my perspiration and wonder why I am here. I think: I could get up and leave and walk up the street and enter a world of air-conditioning. There, I would tap into the hard-edged framework of computers, lined up. Instead of sweat and raw grass, I would smell the perking of wires in my system. I would attempt to gather soul through conversing with machinery. Would my humanity be reflected in their silver screens if I wrote? Or should I stay here and watch the dying butterfly instead? The eternal dilemma. Words spin in my mind. I unbend my body to lie on my back. The grass is in my hair smells fresh like lawn-cut girlhood. Then, even before I had breasts, I would jog down the tarred and black Montana highway, miles from town. The seagulls would wheel overhead, shadowing me as I raced against my own time.

But the birds here in New York are black—crow black, dead black. They rustle and stare with eyes that see . . . what? And here, instead of needles, the trees are heavy with flowers. The white and the pink of their blossoming is furious and violent; their flushed explosions remind me of the blood that floods blue in my veins as I run. Could it really be that all of us—me, the blossoms, and this butterfly—all evolved from the same birthed cell in the sea? I think of the tiny struggles of all the organisms to feed and be fed; I think of the lives that are being born today, at this minute, the hungry mouths that open like wounds to prick at a dry world. I think of the rain that drips slowly into the gutter and flows to the sewer where the rats live and multiply. I think of the golden rainbow overspanning it all: senseless, bloodless, like the rain. I think of the red cardinal who sings and the blue jay who follows it. I think of the holidays and the celebrations which mean so much to us; I think of my friend and the warmth of his brown eyes when they are alight and wrinkled with kindness; I think of all the ways that I shall make him happy. If I concentrate I can almost know what it is like to be him. They say that humans alone among the animals feel true empathy.

After running, I open to tiny upcoming moments of truth. They are so sudden and burp-like that they can be mistaken for a problem in the digestive tract. I turn over on my belly and press my face into the earth. I think of my mother. She said to me: "I wish so much that I was like you. You have such a strong body; you would be such a great marathon runner. When I run with you I feel like you're running downhill and I'm running uphill." I am so grateful for this body; I cannot imagine any other. The pleasures it has given me have been so grave. The weakness of my body is not its constitution, but my being.

That is why I need running. It does more than just strengthen my fibers. It is for the days when I lose track of my being, when I become like a dry leaf, shedding strength in pulses of white frost. Today has been such a day: beautiful, doomful, and hard to endure. Days like this are inevitable for all of us. We must run to strengthen ourselves so we can push against our pain. And indeed, on such days, how I run! My whole body aches in its attempts to be strong. I race with furious strength through the park, feeling threads of euphoria leaping and tightening in my body, sending cool blushes upward. I am as quick and tight as a coiled spring.

Then, at the end, I am collapsed, sick, and gasping for air. My lungs clench and flap like fists. Sometimes the emotion when I finish is such that when I return inside, tears are in my eyes, and I am embarrassed. It feels wrong, sometimes, to be so tender. I wish I were tougher, like when I run. Then, I bypass all the rest with my strong lion legs and whipping body. Running makes me sturdy. Running makes me stand up straight, unblinking and resilient.

I sit back up to face the wing of the cloud that covers the sun, and I see my butterfly again. Suddenly, I realize that it not as sick as I thought, just confused, and wandering. It flounces gaudily through the clover, seeking. A note pulses thrice through the burning sky, and I stand to return home.

Running with Time

Roger Hart

MANKATO, MINNESOTA

Every step brought change. I ran through blizzards, thunderstorms, freezing rain, covered bridges, creeks, campgrounds, cemeteries, city parks, parking lots, a nuclear power plant, county fairs, and, once, a church service. I was chased by goats, geese, a crazed ground hog, guards (the nuclear power plant), a motorcycle gang, an armed man in a pickup, a sheriff's deputy, and dogs both fierce and friendly. I ran when two feet of snow covered the roads and when the wind-chill was thirty below. I ran when it was eighty degrees at seven in the morning. I ran on streets, sidewalks, highways, cinder tracks, dirt roads, golf courses, Lake Erie beaches, bike trails, across yards and along old railroad beds. Seven days a week, twelve months a year.

I gave directions to lost drivers, pushed cars out of snow banks, called the electric company about downed lines and the police about drunks. I saved a burlap bag full of kittens about to be tossed off a bridge, carried turtles from the middle of the road, returned lost wallets, and was the first on the scene of a flipped pickup truck.

I ran the Boston Marathon before women were allowed to enter and before the Kenyans won. I ran before Frank Shorter took the Olympic gold at Munich, before the running boom, nylon shorts, sports drinks, Gore-Tex suits, heart monitors, running watches, and Nikes.

I ate constantly, or so it seemed. My favorite midnight snacks were cookie dough and cold pizza. I loved ice cream and drank large vanilla shakes two at a time.

I measured my life in miles down to the nearest tenth, more than one hundred miles a week, over four hundred a month, four thousand a year, sometimes more.

The smells! From passing cars: pipe tobacco, exhaust fumes, and sometimes the sweet hint of perfume. From the places I passed: frying bacon, pine trees, dead leaves, cut hay, mowed grass, ripe grapes, hot asphalt, rotten apples, stagnant water, wood smoke, charcoal grills, mosquito spray, road-kill. And from myself: sunscreen and sweat.

Some people smiled and waved. A few whistled. Once or twice a woman yelled from a passing car, said I had nice legs. Others, usually teenage boys in sleek, black cars, yelled obscenities, called me names, gave the finger, and mooned me. They threw firecrackers, smoldering cigarettes, pop cans, half-eaten ice cream cones, beer bottles (both full and empty), squirted me with water, drove through puddles to spray me, swerved their cars to force me off the road, swung jumper cables out the window to make me duck, and honked their horns to make me jump.

I saw shooting stars, a family of weasels, a barn fire, a covered wagon heading west, and a couple making love in a pickup; I ran with deer on a golf course, jumped a slow-moving train to get across the tracks, hid in ditches during lightning storms, slid across an intersection during a freezing rain, and dived into Lake Erie to cool off in the middle of a hot run. I drank from garden hoses, gas station water fountains, pop machines, lawn sprinklers, and lemonade stands. I carried toilet paper, two quarters, sometimes a dog biscuit.

I was offered rides by The Chosen Few motorcycle gang, old ladies, drunks, teenagers, truckers, a topless dancer (not topless at the time but close, real close), and a farmer baling hay, but I never accepted a single one. No regrets. (Maybe the dancer.)

I was nervous before races and said I'd quit running them when I wasn't. I won trophies, medals, baskets of apples, bottles of wine, windbreakers, T-shirts, pizza, pewter mugs, running suits, shoes, baseball caps, watches, a railroad spike, and, once, five hundred dollars. Often I didn't win anything, although I never looked at it that way.

My goal was to qualify for the Olympic Trials Marathon, to run faster and farther, to beat other runners.

Did I ever have runner's high? Didn't it get boring? What did I think about? Why did I always look so serious?

Sometimes. Sometimes. Running. I didn't know I did.

I occasionally ran with friends. Long runs of twenty or more miles. Sometimes we laughed until we collapsed, tears and rain running down our faces. Once we got lost during a winter storm and refused to turn around, and one summer we ran by Don King's ranch and were mistaken for two boxers. (We never understood how anyone could mistake our skinny arms for a boxer's, but we loved it, too.) And another time we ran into a church service being held in the middle of a covered bridge, and we were too tired, too inconsiderate, too stubborn to turn around, so we sprinted down the center aisle, dodging the two men with collection plates, and ran out the other end of the bridge while the congregation sang "Praise God from whom all blessings flow . . ."

But most of the time I ran alone.

And the dogs!

I was bitten by a Dalmatian, a terrier, a cocker spaniel, and a red-haired, knee-high mutt. Three of the dogs escaped after drawing blood, but I caught the mutt in mid-air and threw it over my shoulder as its teeth clamped down on my arm. The dog sailed into a telephone pole headfirst and fell to the ground, knocked unconscious. The owner, ignoring the blood running down my arm and dripping onto the sidewalk, screamed at me for killing her dog. But when she stroked the dog's head, it jumped up and bit me again.

I found pliers, purses, golf balls, bolt cutters, billfolds, money (once, over two hundred dollars—returned to an eighteen-year-old boy—no reward, no thanks), tape cassettes, CDs, sunglasses, school books, porn magazines, a Navaho ring, car jacks, a fishing pole, a pair of handcuffs (no key), an eight ball, and a black bra (36C).

I sprinted up long steep hills by the Grand River until I staggered and my heart rate exceeded the two hundred twenty minus my age that doctors said was possible. I ran intervals on a dirt track: twenty quarter-miles under seventy seconds, the last lap in fifty-six flat. I got light-headed, my hands tingled, and once blood vessels in my eye ruptured from the effort.

I ran because I was running towards something, because I was running away, because I was all legs, lungs and heart, because I was afraid of who or what might catch me if I stopped.

One winter, while running twice a day, I was on my way home from a seven-mile run, and I couldn't remember if it was morning or night, if when I finished I would shower and go to work or shower and go to bed. I looked at the horizon and the stars, the passing cars, and the lighted barns for a clue, but I couldn't figure it out.

I lost toenails and pulled muscles. I suffered frostbite, hypothermia, heat exhaustion, sunburn, blisters, dehydration, and tendinitis. I was stung by bees, bitten by black flies, and attacked by red-winged black-birds. Sometimes, after a long run or a speed workout, or after a mara-thon, my legs would be so sore, the Achilles so inflamed, that I could barely walk, and I'd limp or shuffle painfully when going from the couch to the refrigerator or from the front door to the mailbox.

I treated aches with ice and heating pads, sometimes Epsom salts and hot water. I tried medical doctors, surgeons, chiropractors, acupuncturists, podiatrists, sports therapists, trainers and quacks. I was given shots of novocain and cortisone, told to take ibuprofen, tylenol, and aspirin. I was warned that I was ruining my knees, my hips, damaging my feet, breaking down too much blood, that I would suffer arthritis and degenerative joints.

But sometimes it was like floating, like sitting on top of a pair of legs that you didn't think would ever get tired or slow down. It was like the legs were yours and like they weren't. It was like being part animal, a running, flying animal. A horse, a bird. It was like feet kissing the pavement and effortless strides, the body along for the ride. It was like sitting in a Corvette, that monster engine gulping high-octane fuel and turning 6000 rpms, your foot ready to pop the clutch. Like freedom and invincibility.

I had a resting pulse in the low forties and body fat of seven percent or less. I was six foot two, raced at a hundred and forty-eight pounds, and went through a pair of shoes every eight weeks.

Although I ran faster and faster, I never ran fast enough. I failed to qualify for the Olympic Trials. Still, three times I drove for hours and slept in my car to watch others compete for the three Olympic spots.

Then, just as I once stalked other runners, time began stalking me. I started looking over my shoulder and thinking about the marathons I had run instead of thinking about the next race. I slowed down. My body balked at hundred-mile weeks, and it took longer to recover from a hard run. Sometimes when the weather was bad—very hot was always worse than very cold—I took a day off. Sometimes I skipped a day because I was sore or tired. I gained five, seven, ten pounds.

Now, I have a retirement clock. I've turned gray, lost hair, and joined the AARP. I run twenty-five, thirty miles a week. From time to time, I race, no marathons but shorter races, three, four miles, maybe a 10K. I complain that I'm running slower than I once did and make jokes about timing myself with calendars and sundials.

But sometimes when I'm running I'll spot other runners ahead of me and the urge to race comes back, and I'll do my best to catch them. Last fall while I was running in a park, I overheard a high school cross-country coach urge his runners to pass "the old, gray-haired guy." I held them off for nearly a mile although it almost killed me, and, when I had completed circling the park, I ran by the coach and said, "Old guy, my ass."

But my ass is getting older along with all the other parts. When I fantasize about one more marathon, the fantasy seldom lasts more than a day. Fast marathons, hundred-mile weeks, ten-kilometer races under thirty-one minutes are things of the past.

And what did I learn from running eighty thousand miles and hundreds of races, being the first to cross the finish line and once or twice not crossing it at all, those runs on icy roads in winter storms and those cool fall mornings when the air was ripe with the smell of grapes, my feet softly ticking against the pavement?

I learned I was alive and it felt good. God, it feels so good.